SCHOOL HAPPENS

MICHELE ROBINSON

WRITTEN WITH RHONA SILVERBUSH AND SAMI PLOTKIN

authorHOUSE

AuthorHouse™
1663 Liberty Drive
Bloomington, IN 47403
www.authorhouse.com
Phone: 1 (800) 839-8640

Published by AuthorHouse 05/29/2020

ISBN: 978-1-7283-5139-1 (sc)
ISBN: 978-1-7283-5138-4 (e)

CONTENTS

FOREWORD BY SAKI DODELSON

Every appliance—from the most simple to the most complex—is packaged with an instruction manual: how to get started, how to use it and how to troubleshoot problems. Yet, when it comes to our kids' education, there's no manual, no "how to" section, and no FAQ page to reference. How ironic that education, an area that has far-reaching impact on lifelong success, comes with no quick-start booklet. Every individual with a child in their life is left to figure things out and draw their own conclusions based on conversations with friends and web searches. In the best case, we are guided in the right direction and our children make it through the school system with flying colors. In the worst case, we are left to pick up the pieces of a child robbed of her education and her future. In most cases, though, we learn on the job and do our best to guide the child. In hindsight we wish someone would have advised us so that we didn't have to lose valuable time and resources in the process.

It's not ok for a child to fall through the cracks. It's not ok for anyone to feel that opportunity is reserved for the privileged. Education is a basic human right. With it, doors open. Deprived of it, confidence plummets and the road to a fulfilling future remains elusive. In the past two decades, as part of my work leading ed-tech companies, I have had an inside view to our public-school system, and in most cases, our nation's educators care deeply about our kids. We need to better understand the insides of the system so that we can maximize the partnership.

We owe it to our children to do our utmost to maximize those thirteen remarkable years they are in school. This book will walk you through the process. Finally! A guidebook to help you help the child in your life stride through the confusing hallways of schools and emerge victorious. In this book, Michele Robinson, an expert in the field of education, tells you how to navigate and prepare for each phase of your child's education: what to expect, what services you are entitled to and how to secure them, and how to address diverse learning styles.

In the decade that I have known Michele, she has lived and breathed passion for kids and their right to an education that brings out their best and prepares them for a productive future. For 25 years she has worked with students, their parents, teachers and school administrators, giving her a powerful 360° perspective. I have always found her insight to be perceptive and invaluable, and it has been an honor to work together with her, helping millions of kids. In this book she'll give you a clear path forward based on her rich experience. Whether you are just starting this journey or already a few years in, you will find this book invaluable and lifechanging.

PREFACE

YOUR CHILD CAN ROCK SCHOOL: A K-12 TOOLKIT FOR EVERY PARENT

If you are holding this book in your hands, I know that somewhere in your life there is a fantastic, unique, well-loved child whom you wish to support on his or her educational journey. You are probably this child's proud parent, but you may also be a grandparent or guardian or other caring, concerned presence in that child's life. Perhaps the child has done beautifully in school and is suddenly slipping; perhaps he or she has never performed well and has suffered snowballing loss of self-esteem over time; or perhaps the child is doing fine but you'd like to make his or her experience in school the best and most fun it can be. Whatever your child's story is, this book can help you shape his or her educational experience into an adventure that helps your child become a smart, capable, successful adult.

I realize that parents are working harder than ever and have less time, fewer financial resources and far less energy to devote to figuring out their children's learning pitfalls and remedying them.

Parents could really use a comprehensive guideline that lays out:

- "the big picture" about school from K-12;
- the goals of the US educational system for our students;
- how we measure our children's progress;
- how parents can use this info to help their children;
- the different ways in which humans learn;
- best practices for homework and in-class learning;
- obstacles to learning; and
- ways to determine whether additional supports for learning are needed and how to acquire them.

If you had this information and could implement a targeted approach to your child's learning that was easy, intuitive and effective, I know you surely would.

You can.

In an ideal world, school would be exciting and inspiring for every child. It would help each child acquire the skills needed to thrive in life. It would allow each child to address his or her own individual challenges and emerge from them with confidence and high self-esteem. And of course, learning would come easily for each one. Unfortunately, even the best of schools cannot achieve this goal for every child. But here's the good news: as a parent, there is a lot you can do to make your child's K-12 years successful, enjoyable, and rewarding. The chapters that follow will show you how.

INTRODUCTION

I feel that many parents or caregivers want to help their kids in school and don't know how. They feel helpless. This book can change that. If parents had a guide that navigates all the things that they will experience at each grade and can help their kids prepare, know what to ask at parent conferences, how to get help if they feel their child may need extra attention, be struggling with a learning disability, or not being challenged, this book will guide them and give them options. Ive been very fortunate to work in an industry of supplemental education and assessment that allowed me to work side by side with parents, educators, district leadership and community leaders to shape the future and ensure every student has the opportunity to be successful and have options for college or career. With an intentional focus on life readiness beyond just getting a job. Ive always felt that if parents knew what to expect and how to help their kids they would.

ACKNOWLEDGEMENTS

I want to thank the following people for their love, support, contributions and encouragement that made this dream possible. I have been very fortunate over the last 20+ years to be in a career that I love. I have the opportunity to help so many families and educators to change the world by helping kids make the most of school to ensure they have options for college and career. I was fortunate to learn early on that opportunities are endless if you can envision exactly what you want your life to look like and are willing to work really hard to make it happen. My mom calls it "running the movie."

I have this extraordinary mother (Reesa Manning) that has always been my biggest champion and also the most extraordinary human you could ever meet.. My husband (John), who has supported and loved me unconditionally in the best and worst of times. Its been 25 years and my greatest wish is that we are lucky enough to get 50 more. My inlaws, (Cheri and Veryl) who are just the best inlaws a person could ever ask for. I know how lucky I got.

My co -writers Rhona and Sami, Mentors: Joan Evans, BJ Mettle, Saki Dodelson, and my friend and colleague Susan Edmiston who gave me the exact push and help in the final stages of completing the book that I needed. Thank you!

One additional note: To all the people I have had the incredible opportunity to manage/ coach over the years and have been part of my teams. My greatest passion and joy comes from having the priviledge to help people see their potential and feel part of something bigger than themselves. It's a gift to do a job that you love and have a positive impact on the world by harnessing the collective energy that can only happen when you bring remarkable, talented, and driven people together and use intention, passion, and grit to overcome every obstacle and achieve greatness. I am forever grateful to these teams and individuals who motivated me every day to be the very best and never give up when you know that what you do everyday- matters. Thank you!

SECTION ONE

ALL ABOUT SCHOOL

Times have changed since the one-room schoolhouse where the teacher wielded a ruler, and the children of all ages recited aloud. Thank goodness.

Times have also changed since you and I were kids, which is why I think that if you're looking to support your child's educational efforts, it would be helpful for you to understand how the school experience has evolved, what the goals are for today's students, how school are trying to meet those goals, and how they determine whether they are succeeding.

So, this first section is all about school! Pack up your tuna sandwich, your apple, and your milk carton, strap on your helmet, hop aboard your Razor Scooter, and let's go!

CHAPTER ONE

WHAT HAPPENS IN SCHOOL: A GRADE-BY-GRADE GUIDE (SCHOOL 101)

Imagine that you have walked your kindergartner to school on her first day. When you actually get there, you see a large institutional building with a play yard and bright red doors. But in my mind's eye, you have walked your child right up to the edge of a big, empty hole in the ground! What you're looking at is your child's education, waiting to be built.

Your child is the General Contractor. She's got a whole team of builders to help her (including you!), but ultimately, she will have to put in place every slab and every brick of that education herself. This chapter will help you understand what those bricks are made of, how they fit together, and what you can do to support your builder on the job. Seeing the big picture will put into context for you all the information that follows in this book.

HOW TO USE THIS CHAPTER

This is the longest chapter in the book. It's also the densest. But that's OK - you can choose how much (if any!) of it you want to read: When taken as a whole, this chapter gives you, the parent, the Big Picture about the arc of your child's K-12 education with detail about the skills and concepts being tackled in each grade. But if you wish, you can jump straight to the sections that describe what's happening in your child's current grade and use the pointers you find there to help your child get the most out of his year.

> ### GLEasy
>
> You'll hear educators bandy about the initials "GLEs" (usually in the plural, as here). This just stands for "Grade Level Expectations." It's the official set of skills and knowledge (the educational standards) your child is expected to master in a particular grade.

> **READ!**
>
> What I'm about to say applies to every child in every grade:
>
> *A child who does not like to read will always struggle in school.*
>
> I will be saying this is different ways throughout this book, because the ability to read well is the single most important factor in your child's academic success. It is important not only to help your child read well, but also to help him develop a love of reading. I will discuss ways to accomplish this throughout the book.

ESSENTIAL BUILDING BLOCKS FOR SUCCESS, GRADE BY GRADE

Whether you live in Arkansas or Alaska, your child's school career takes the following trajectory: In kindergarten through second grade, your child is absorbing the basics for learning; in third through fifth, he is taking these skills to a higher level, progressing to higher-level thinking and preparing for middle school; in sixth through eighth, your child is learning to make more complex analyses and formally express them; and in high school he is being prepared for the larger world, whether that means college or the work force.

Let's break this down. What I am about to describe in this chapter is the general way in which your child's education develops between the day she enters kindergarten and the day she's handed her high school diploma.

Kindergarten

Your kindergartner is literally laying the foundation for his entire education! First of all, kindergarten is where children learn how to go to school: "Here's how we hang up our coats when we arrive; Here's how we behave in the classroom; Here's how we work on projects with our friends..." But it has become more than this; it is now your child's first academic experience as well, at least the first one where there are expectations and assessments. Certain Language Arts concepts must be firmly rooted by the end of the year, forming the basis for the single most important skill he needs to master in elementary school - READING.

By the end of the year, your successful kindergartener:

- Listens to stories and answers simple questions about the main idea or message;
- Recognizes and names the letters of the alphabet;
- Knows the sounds of the letters of the alphabet;
- Understands concepts of print (how print is organized and read);
- Understands small numbers, quantities, and simple shapes in their environment;

- Develops a sense of properties and patterns with numbers, shapes and sets;
- Describes, sorts and re-sorts objects using a variety of attributes such as shape, size, and position.

How you can nurture this growth:

Read to your child. And then enhance the learning by asking questions: Who is the main character in the story? What do you think is going to happen next and why? Which kid in the illustration do you think is Sparky and which kid is Lois? How could you tell?

Investigate the book. Before you read, ask your child: Which way should I hold the book? Can you point to the title? Where should I start to read?

Invest in some foam bathtub letters (the kind that stick to the tile when wet). My friend's son wrote his first 'sentence' in foam bathtub letters: BUGZ AR OCAY (He's a budding entomologist!)

Introduce sight words. Take a look at the box about sight words on Appendix A. They will be a key building block for your kindergartner!

Get her to help clean up! Sorting toys into bins by size, color, or shape is a great math activity – and it keeps her room neat.

Invite him to make dinner. Let your child do the measuring for recipes.

Go on a 'Shape Hunt.' Look around your house for different shapes. When your child masters 2D shapes, start looking for cubes, spheres, and rectangular prisms. You'll be surprised how hard it can be to find a cone shape - I bet your kid will find the first one.

Play the Game of Phonemic Awareness with Your 3 – 7 Year Old

"Phonemic awareness" is simply the ability to recognize and manipulate the individual sounds in words. This ability is essential for decoding words in order to read and write them. You can build your child's phonemic awareness by playing fun games throughout your day. Here are a few examples:

- <u>Active Listening</u> - Have your child close her eyes, then make a sound (close a door, open a cabinet, click a ball point pen, etc.). See if she can identify the sound.

- <u>Silliness with Sounds</u> - Take turns replacing words in rhymes or songs with nonsense ("Mary had a little car..."); saying words in the wrong order ("And the last little weeeee went 'Piggy, piggy, piggy' all the way home!"); or swapping onset sounds ("Little Bo Sheep has lost her peep, and doesn't know fair to wind them."). Warning: this game has been known to cause severe giggling.

- <u>Word Onset Games</u> - The onset of a word is its beginning sound. Try a game in which you pick up an object – let's say, a hat – and say a magic spell. Pretend to change the hat into a cat. Give the object to the child and let her change it into something else by magically changing the word's first sound.

- <u>Rhyming Games</u> - One mom I know rhymes with her child on the subway. She or Eli will just start in during an everyday conversation: Eli says, "Mommy, I ate all my grapes, I want some more." She gives him a conspiratorial look and says, "Well, I guess we better stop at the STORE." Recognizing the game, he grins and replies, "I will eat them before we get out the DOOR!" "But what if they fall on the FLOOR?" "Then I will be so mad I will ROAR!!"

- <u>Clap the Syllables</u> - Teach your child to clap out the syllables in words. Then challenge her to find out 'which word is longer' (i.e., which has more syllables) by clapping them out: "Which is longer, 'par-ty' or 'train'"?

Sight Words on Site

Remember that big empty pit your child faced when she came to school the first day? Well, sight words are one of the key ingredients she'll need to mix the cement for her foundation.

Sight words are words your child recognizes automatically, without sounding them out. Beginning readers are working hard to sound words out, so the more words they can read on sight, the more confident they feel. There are different lists of sight words, but they vary only slightly. The most commonly used list was compiled by Edward Dolch in 1936. Dolch's list is comprised of 220 "service words" that have to be easily recognized in order to achieve reading fluency in English. Many of the words can't be sounded out (think of 'the' and 'out'). There is a separate 95-word list of nouns, which are more easily taught because they can be tied to images.

The Dolch list is divided into sections by grade level. You can find a complete list of the Dolch sight words by grade as well as the list of nouns at the back of this book (Appendix A). It's easy to make up your own flash cards, which you can practice with your child for 10 minutes every day. Boxed sets of sight word flashcards are also widely available online or in the bookstore. You can even get them on DVD!

Sight words are the perfect place to start implementing the concept of "chunking" - breaking down a large body of information and learning it in doable chunks (more about chunking in Chapter Three). Take your list of 52 kindergarten words and tackle five or ten at a time. Let your child be the Sight Word Sleuth - ask him to scout out his sight words at the supermarket and in the mall. When you're in the car, you can start a competition with him to see who can be first to spot ten sight words on signs and billboards. If your child learns five sight words a week, he will have mastered the kindergarten list well before the end of the year. If that happens, forge on with the next set of words. Or go back and start at the beginning - the reinforcement will help strengthen that foundation your child is building. Dolch's original recommendation was that children learn all the words by the end of third grade. In today's competitive environment, however, many educators are speeding up the rate at which kids are seeing the words appear on the Word Wall in their classrooms.

The more sight words your child recognizes, the better. First of all (and very importantly), knowing sight words will mean that your child has fewer words per sentence to laboriously sound out. She will be able to make sense of each sentence and will feel more successful and less frustrated during this challenging process of learning to read. Less frustration means greater enjoyment . . . which sets your child up to be a willing and even enthusiastic reader . . . which sets your child up to better succeed in all subjects in school. It also paves the way for how she'll read later on. Think about your own reading . . . almost every word you read is a sight word, isn't it? By the time you're an adult, it's only rarely that you actually decode a word using phonetics!

First Grade

Remember how your child laid the foundation for that school building in kindergarten? Well, imagine construction of the building's first floor in time-lapse photography - that's how fast your child's reading skills will progress in first grade! If she's on track, you will see her march through several reading levels during the course of the year. Many first graders start out the year with books that have only one or two sentences per page and finish the year reading chapter books! You'll see that reflected in the first-grade building blocks:

- Identifies the beginning, middle, and ending sounds of words;
- Uses sound/symbol relationships as visual cues for decoding;
- Generates and blends sounds from consonants, long and short vowels, spelling patterns;
- Identifies and classifies common words from within basic categories;
- Generates ideas, records them in written form, publishes writing with help;
- Understands and uses the concept of ones and tens in the place value number system;
- Orders counting numbers, compares their relative magnitudes, and represents numbers on a number line;
- Learns to do simple problem solving with real life situations.

How you can nurture this growth:

Focus on sight words! First grade is a very big year for reading. Make sure your child is mastering those sight words. Take a look at the Sight Words box above.

Help your child achieve fluency. Model fluency by reading to your child with expression. Give her many opportunities to read aloud to you for practice. See the box on page 14 for more suggestions.

Tap into your child's great loves. Provide your child with book at his "just right level" as assessed by your teacher. If you are not sure which system your school uses, check in with the teacher. (It's probably "Lexile.") And here's the key: Give him books he loves! Whether he's into SpongeBob, comic books, or the life cycle of worms, honor that preference (even if it's something you wouldn't have chosen) and provide books that will make him love reading.

Encourage writing at home. Ask your child to help you out by writing down the items for your grocery list. Have her write her own thank you notes or party invitations, even if she's just signing her own name at first. (See Appendix B for an extensive list of ways you can incorporate writing into your child's day as well as for motivating writing projects you can do at home.)

Become the First Bank of Mommy/Daddy. Handling money is a very motivating way to begin to understand numbers (particularly the concept of place value). Let your child save up coins, then count them out and trade for larger coins or bills. Take her to open a real bank account, and make sure she's signed up to receive paper statements in the mail.

Sneak in the math facts. Work math facts into your everyday activities. Make a game of it when you're in transit ("Let's see if we can do +2 up to twelve before we get to the corner!"); make up +1, +2, and +3 flash cards and offer a small reward if she beats her own time getting through them. Don't forget to let her time you on them as well - she'll benefit from the repetition, and being in charge of the stopwatch makes it fun.

Second Grade

My young friend Jared was recently explaining to me over ice cream how big he is now that he's in second grade. He feels very comfortable in school - he feels like he's handling everything they're throwing at him. And while he doesn't know it, he's on to something: the second grade curriculum is really a continuation of what your child worked on in first grade; this year is about moving toward a deeper understanding and mastery of the skills your child has been honing for the last two years.

- Blends sound components into words;
- Decodes two-syllable words, regular multi-syllable words, and words with plurals;
- Writes legibly and generates ideas before writing on self-selected topics and assigned tasks;
- Orally recounts experiences or present stories and speaks clearly;
- Uses parts of speech, capitalization, and punctuation correctly in writing;
- Reads with fluency, accuracy and expression;
- Decodes complex word families and recognizes 300 high frequency words;
- Understands place value and number relationships in addition and subtraction;
- Classifies shapes and sees relationships among them;
- Measures quantities with appropriate units;
- Collects and analyzes data and verifies answers.

How you can nurture this growth:

Keep up the writing at home. Kids love to get mail, and you can take advantage of that. Often, when kids discover that they will be rewarded by something in the mailbox, they are motivated to write all kinds of letters (notes to grandma, queries to the Customer Service department of their favorite toy manufacturer, replies to letters they get from the tooth fairy (hint, hint), etc.)

Work on fluency. See the box on fluency below. Your child must be able to read confidently by the end of next year. Use this time to build his reading skills.

Skip count for fun. Kai, a second grader I know, is entertained during his nightly tooth brushing by his father, who skip counts with him. They started with 10s and 5s (the easiest), graduated to 2s, and are now working on 3s. Skip counting prepares kids for the multiplication that's coming next year. When Kai taught his friend Julia to skip count, she said, "Let's skip and skip count." Now, every time they see each other they skip and skip count until they fall down out of breath with skipping and laughter.

Fluency: An Easy Indicator of Reading Skills

When your child's teacher assesses his reading skills, she has many tools at hand and uses a detailed method of measuring accuracy, fluency, and comprehension at her particular reading level. The easiest of these indicators for you to observe at home is fluency.

Fluency is the ability to read smoothly and accurately with appropriate expression. A child must be able to read fluently (both silently and out loud) in order to understand the text. In other words, fluency may seem like a cosmetic thing, but it directly affects comprehension!

If your child is having trouble with fluency, here are some strategies you can use at home:

Model fluent reading for your child. Even if the book is not so exciting to you, read with interest and expression.

- Read aloud with your child, allowing him to match his voice up with yours.
- Have your child practice reading the same sentence or short passage several times in a row.
- Remind her to pause between sentences and phrases.
- Give him books with predictable vocabulary and clear rhythmic patterns that are hard not to hear (Dr. Seuss is a great example).

"First you learn to read, then you read to learn."

I'm sure you've heard that commonplace, and guess what? It's true - and the big turnaround moment happens in third grade. Study after study shows that if children are not strong readers by the end of third grade, they never catch up. And since they are henceforth 'reading to learn,' that means they will fall behind in every subject, not just Language Arts. If you have a third grader, this is the year to make sure your child's reading skills are on track!

Third Grade

Third grade is a big year. In the imaginary school building your child's been constructing, the electrical system needs to start being connected: Kids are transitioning from spending much of their time getting practice at basic skills, learning facts, and memorizing sight words and math facts, to doing tasks that involve critical thinking. It's also a key moment for math. Math facts that are not solidified during this year will be a monster to deal with down the line. Here's what your third grader is working on:

- Discusses meanings of words and develops vocabulary through real world experiences, reading independently, and using reference books;
- Distinguishes between cause and effect, fact and opinion, main idea, supporting details, and making inferences;

- Deepens understanding of place value with addition, subtraction, multiplication and division of whole numbers;
- Identifies, describes, and applies division and multiplication as inverse operations;
- Represents number relationships with fractions, including fractions greater than one.

How you can nurture this growth:

Get in her face with the times tables! You will notice that the simple bullet point 'memorizes entire multiplication table' does not appear in the list of general building blocks above. As I've mentioned, somehow these essential math facts have been left largely to the child and parent to handle. Post them next to the computer, in the car, on the bathroom mirror. Make the 6x table a requirement before dessert is served. Say the 9x table before you tuck her in. Put the times tables up on the wall she looks at as she goes to sleep. Make it impossible for her *not* to see it. Let me repeat that one: Put the times tables up on the wall she looks at as she goes to sleep. Make it impossible for her *not* to see it.

Again, this is the time for "chunking" - let's work on the 2x table for a while before moving on to the 3x table. Let's make sure your child knows both the 2x and 3x tables before moving on to the 4x table, and knows all three before moving on to the 5x table. And there's plenty of time in the school year to start over again from the 2x (or work backwards from the 12x) table ...more than once. Apply the tables to real life - how many pairs of nickels do we need to buy this 50-cent item? You're eight - how old will you be when you're twice your age? Three times your age? How many times your age will you need to be to be older than your Dear Ole Dad is now? Memorizing the times tables now will help her in middle school and high school more than any math concept she learns in all of elementary school.

> Put the
> times tables
> up on the wall she looks
> at as she goes to sleep.
> Make it impossible for
> her *not* to see it.

Request a customized book review. Show an interest in what your child is reading for fun. Ask questions about the book that will prompt him to think critically ("Who do you think *did* steal the baseball? Why do you think so?" "Should Sophia talk with a grown-up about her problem?" "Why do you think Andy was mean to his best friend?

How YOU Can Use the Multiplication Tables to Save the World

In the course of my work, I meet many high school dropouts. When I ask the kids why they drop out, I get the same answer time and again: they feel overwhelmingly unsuccessful. Further probing shows that this feeling actually begins not in high school but in middle school. A contributor to these young people's feelings of inadequacy that we cannot ignore is MATH. And if you look a little closer, you'll discover it's not just any math that is the straw that breaks the camel's back, it's ALGEBRA. Lots and lots of kids nationwide just can't pass Algebra. The problem is so ubiquitous that most states' standards now set Algebra in 8th grade, even though it was once a high school subject. Why? Because if they fail it in 8th grade, they'll still have time to take it again.

I'm not kidding. That's really why. Appalling, right?

Doesn't it seem like there should be a better solution? Well, there is! If we look at why kids are failing Algebra, we discover that it's because they don't know their third grade math facts! They also don't understand a good deal of the material that relies on those facts, such as decimals, fractions, and percentages. Without all that foundation, no kid is going to pass Algebra, no matter how many times he takes it.

The solution is obvious: help the kids learn their math facts and other early algebraic concepts when they're supposed to. Then more kids will pass math, find it fun instead of dreary, stay in school, find better jobs, become more productive citizens, and voila! We've saved the world.

You can do your part by using your Superparent Powers. Make sure your kid:

- has his math facts memorized and understands fractions by the end of 3rd grade,
- has mastered the four math operations (see Appendix C) by the end of 5th grade,
- knows the rules for negative numbers by the end of 6th grade, and
- understands the relationships among fractions, decimals and percents by the end of 7th grade.

What parents can do in the home is focus in on the key things that kids really must know to support the next level of math - and reinforce, reinforce, reinforce so that the child has the strong, deep understanding of the concept.

And Don't Forget Fractions!

"The subject of fractions is able to prepare students for the level of generalization that is necessary for understanding algebraic concepts," writes George Brown in the internet magazine CBS Interactive Business Network, "Fractions should not be the bane of algebraic manipulations, but rather a familiar subject providing a foundation, which makes the understanding of algebra possible. If algebra is for everyone, then all students must first become familiar and fluent with fractions."

The best way to help kids "get" math and enjoy it is to make it part of your everyday life and make it fun. See Appendix C for an extensive list of fun, engaging games and activities you can do with your kids at home, on the road, even while doing chores and errands.

READING FOR READINESS: Start your own SSR

Recently, some teachers have incorporated SSR (Sustained Silent Reading) into the school day. Sometimes they use catchy acronyms like DEAR (Drop Everything and Read) or FUR (Free Uninterrupted Reading), but the idea is the same: a set time each day when kids get to read for fun. If your child isn't doing SSR in school, you could consider making 15 to 45 minutes of reading for fun a daily whole-family practice. Advocates point out that SSR engenders a positive attitude toward reading and improved scores in reading comprehension and vocabulary.

Fourth Grade

Fourth grade is all about writing. And by writing, I don't mean penmanship - welcome to the age of computers. No, I mean that your child is ready to take those critical thinking skills he developed in third grade and express them on paper. Almost every state gives an independent writing proficiency exam in fourth grade. This is also the year in which most states test kids in science for the first time. Here are the building blocks:

- Analyzes literature through plot, character, actions, figurative language and author's tone;
- Writes to reflect purpose and audience;
- Creates a paragraph with a topic sentence, supporting sentences and concluding statement;
- Re-writes or revises written work;
- Describes and compares simple fractions and decimals;
- Collects, represents, and analyzes data to answer questions;
- Represents number relationships and solves problems involving probabilities.

How you can nurture this growth:

Encourage the brain dump! Kids are taught the skill of writing and revising to a much greater degree today than when we were young. Encourage your child to get all her ideas down on the paper first and worry about refining them later.

Use the web to conceptualize. No, not the worldwide web, the "idea web": Think of your child's concept as the spider. Whatever your child's story is about - his cat, a fireman, Superman - is sitting there right in the middle of the web. Then add each idea - Superman has cool powers; Superman helps people - as a few words on a line coming off that web. Another version of this is an "idea tree." The main concept is the trunk and the ideas form the branches.

Stress the structure. When your child is working on a writing assignment, make sure he can tell you what the structure of the piece will be. It should include an introductory sentence or paragraph, at least three supporting sentences or paragraphs, and a concluding sentence or paragraph.

Leveled Reading: State of the Art Reading for Elementary School

Remember when you learned to read? Probably not - I can't. But what I do remember is that all the kids in my class sat in a big circle and took turns reading from the same text. Things have changed a lot since then. Current thinking is that kids need to practice reading at their own individual levels. That means your child is given 'just right books' at school to practice reading from. 'Just right' means a child can read the book with fluency, comprehension, and 90 to 96% accuracy (depending on which expert you ask), i.e., if your child's teacher assesses for 96% accuracy, that means he will not get more than 4 words wrong out of 100 when reading a 'just right' book.

The idea is that when reading independently, your child should not find the book very challenging - He's reading for practice, and you don't want him to struggle or make guesses. When he reads with you or a teacher, he can be reading at a higher level, because an adult is there to scaffold (i.e., provide individualized educational supports for the child to succeed in) the work.

Supporting this system at home can be a little daunting. That's because there are several different systems for 'leveling' books (grouping books together in a sequence of levels for children of different reading abilities). If you want to provide your child with extra books at home at his just right level, you will discover it's not so easy. Many books are marked with only one of the many leveling systems, and some are not marked at all. A helpful resource is the Book Wizard page on the Scholastic website (http://bookwizard.scholastic.com/tbw/homePage.do). This page of the site is meant for teachers, but many parents find it helpful in choosing books for their kids - especially when that Scholastic flyer comes home in your kid's backpack. Again, in order to use it effectively, you'll need to know which leveling system your school uses. Most likely it's one of the four the site will sort for (which is most likely Lexile).

Fifth Grade

Fifth graders are preparing for what may be the biggest transition in their entire education - the shift to middle school. Their workload is upped significantly this year so they won't be completely shell-shocked next year. Here are the major building blocks your child will need to master to be ready for the greater demands that will be made on her:

- Identifies and analyzes the characteristics of non-fiction, fiction, drama and poetry;
- Describes author's purpose and describes how an author's perspective influences the text;
- Reads and organizes information from multiple sources for a variety of purposes- (i.e., interviews, reports);
- Consistently shows proficiency in language use and routinely and carefully rereads writing to revise and improve it;
- Shows increased facility with the four math operations with positive fractions, decimals and positive and negative numbers;
- Relates equivalent fractions and decimals with and without models, including location on a number line;
- Uses grids, tables, graphs, and charts to record and analyze data.

How you can nurture this growth:

Help her cement her study skills. This is the single biggest thing you can do for your kid in fifth grade. Study skills will be absolutely critical for handling the multi-course program of middle school. Don't worry - in Chapter Six, I will discuss key study skills in detail and how to help your child adopt them as lifelong habits.

Sixth Grade

This year, your 10 or 11 year old will most likely go from the school he's attended for years, where he knows scores of children, to a whole new building where he knows very few of the kids; from having three or fewer teachers who cover academic subjects, who knew each child as a person and supported the whole child, to having a different teacher for every class; and from having a safe classroom that is his home at school most of the day to traveling from room to room all day long. He'll go from being one the oldest kids in a school to being at the bottom of the totem pole at a time when some students are physically fully adolescent, while others still look like little kids. It's a *huge* adjustment academically and socially. While handling all this, your middle-schooler is expected to do some serious work on his education construction site:

- Cites textual evidence to support analysis of what a text says explicitly as well as inferences drawn from the text (These days, 50% of elementary school texts are supposed to be nonfiction; this percentage increases throughout middle school and reaches 70% or more in high school.);
- Determines a theme or central idea of a text and describes how it is conveyed through particular details; provides a summary of the text distinct from personal opinions or judgments;
- Determines the meaning of words and phrases, including figurative and connotative meanings; analyzes the impact of word choice on meaning and tone;

- Analyzes how a portion of a text fits into its overall structure and contributes to the development of the theme, setting, or plot;
- Explains how an author develops point of view;
- Writes multi-paragraph essays using a variety of sentence structures;
- Masters the four math operations with whole numbers, positive fractions, and positive and negative integers;
- Uses addition and multiplication of fractions to calculate the probabilities for compound events;
- Uses letters for numbers in formulas involving geometric shapes and in ratios for the unknown part of an expression;
- Adds and subtracts fractions and decimals fluently and verifies the reasonableness of results.

How you can nurture this growth:

Speak up. It's a turning point for kids, going from one school to the next. Some kids are bound to get lost in the shuffle, and if your child is one of them, then squeaky wheel technology is called for. Most teachers genuinely care about their students and want to nurture their growth. But due to ongoing budget cuts and a competitive global environment, today's teachers are often overloaded with large class sizes, huge course loads, and a ton of material to teach. If a parent has contact with the teacher, there's no question that the teacher's awareness level will increase with regard to that particular kid. See tips for parent conferences in Appendix D.

Seventh Grade

Just when your child is through getting used to middle school, preparation for high school begins! Take a look at the high-level thinking your child is expected to do in seventh grade:

English Language Arts:

- Cite textual evidence to support analysis of what the text says explicitly as well as inferences drawn from the text;
- Determine a theme or central idea of a text and analyze its development over the course of the text; provide an objective summary of the text;
- Analyze how particular elements of a story or drama interact (e.g., how setting shapes the characters or plot);
- Determine the meaning of words and phrases as they are used in a text, including figurative and connotative meanings; analyze the impact of rhymes and other repetitions of sounds (e.g., alliteration) on a specific verse or stanza of a poem or section of a story or drama;
- Analyze how a drama's or poem's form or structure (e.g., soliloquy, sonnet) contributes to its meaning;
- Analyze how an author develops and contrasts the points of view of different characters or narrators in a text;
- Compare and contrast a written story, drama, or poem to its audio, filmed, staged, or multimedia version, analyzing the effects of techniques unique to each medium (e.g., lighting, sound, color, or camera focus and angles in a film);

- Compare and contrast a fictional portrayal of a time, place, or character and a historical account of the same period as a means of understanding how authors of fiction use or alter history;
- Write essays with a thesis statement and supporting details using literary devices such as metaphors, analogies and symbols.

Math:

- Analyze proportional relationships and use them to solve real-world and mathematical problems;
- Apply and extend previous understandings of operations with fractions to add, subtract, multiply, and divide rational numbers;
- Use properties of operations to generate equivalent expressions;
- Solve real-life and mathematical problems using numerical and algebraic expressions and equations;
- Draw, construct and describe geometrical figures and describe the relationships between them;
- Solve real-life and mathematical problems involving angle measure, area, surface area, and volume;
- Use random sampling to draw inferences about a population;
- Draw informal comparative inferences about two populations;
- Investigate chance processes and develop, use, and evaluate probability models.

How you can nurture this growth:

For the next two years, Algebra is king. As you can see from the timeline I've provided throughout this chapter, your child has been learning algebraic concepts from Day One of Kindergarten. But most likely, your child will take what is officially called "pre-algebra" this year. Algebra is *the* biggest stumbling block for kids in middle school. Take this year to make sure your child has all her mathematical ducks in order. If you're not sure what that means, make an appointment to meet with your child's teacher to find out if your budding mathematician is on course to be Algebra-ready.

> "Success in algebra often correlates to success in college, so it is very important for today's students to do their best with this critical subject."
>
> - Morgan Griffith, Center Director, Federal Way Sylvan Learning Center

Eighth Grade:

Eighth grade is the second grade of middle school. Whaaaaat? Just as second grade cemented the skills taught in Kindergarten and first grade in preparation for the shift to "reading to learn," eighth grade cements what your child has learned throughout middle school in preparation for high school.

Your child is examining texts in greater depth and in a broader context; she has completed her foundation in math and has moved on to her very first course in upper level math - Algebra! Check out what your 8th-grader will be able to do by the end of the year:

<u>English Language Arts</u>

- Cite the textual evidence that most strongly supports an analysis of what the text says explicitly as well as inferences drawn from the text;
- Determine a theme or central idea of a text and analyze its development over the course of the text, including its relationship to the characters, setting, and plot; provide an objective summary of the text;
- Analyze how particular lines of dialogue or incidents in a story or drama propel the action, reveal aspects of a character, or provoke a decision;
- Determine the meaning of words and phrases as they are used in a text, including figurative and connotative meanings; analyze the impact of specific word choices on meaning and tone, including analogies or allusions to other texts;
- Compare and contrast the structure of two or more texts and analyze how the differing structure of each text contributes to its meaning and style;
- Analyze how differences in the points of view of the characters and the audience or reader (e.g., created through the use of dramatic irony) create such effects as suspense or humor;
- Analyze the extent to which a filmed or live production of a story or drama stays faithful to or departs from the text or script, evaluating the choices made by the director or actors;
- Analyze how a modern work of fiction draws on themes, patterns of events, or character types from myths, traditional stories, or religious works such as the Bible, including describing how the material is rendered new;
- By the end of the year, read and comprehend literature, including stories, dramas, and poems, at the high end of the grades 6 - 8 text complexity level independently and proficiently;
- Develop a research plan to gather, analyze and evaluate information;
- Locate and use primary and secondary sources.

<u>Math</u>

- Work with radicals and integer exponents;
- Understand the connections between proportional relationships, lines, and linear equations;
- Analyze and solve linear equations and pairs of simultaneous linear equations;
- Define, evaluate, and compare functions;
- Use functions to model relationships between quantities;
- Understand congruence and similarity using physical models, transparencies, or geometry software;
- Understand and apply the Pythagorean Theorem;
- Solve real-world and mathematical problems involving volume of cylinders, cones and spheres;
- Investigate patterns of association in data containing more than one variable.

How you can support this growth:

Engage Guidance Counselors. Parents who meet with their kids' counselors and help forge a path of a relationship with the counselor are giving their kids a leg up. A counselor can make a huge impact on high school readiness, both academically and socially.

High School:

Wow, your kid has made it to the big leagues! From here on out, everything changes. Your child's education at this stage is much more individualized. If you think of our construction site analogy, hopefully by now your child has built a strong foundation and a well-designed structure, complete with electrical and plumbing. Now it's time to plaster the walls, pick the linoleum tiles, and choose paint colors for the classroom walls.

At this level it's much more difficult to break down essential building blocks by grade, since kids are focusing on their own interests (one kid wants mosaics on all the walls) and working at varying paces (another kid is waiting for a long-overdue shipment of fluorescent light fixtures that's holding up construction). The goal now is college or career readiness in whatever form that will take for your child.

That being said, your state may still have certain course requirements a child must fulfill in order to graduate. Most high school students will have to take some type of exit exam as well. Here are the basics:

English Language Arts

In almost any state, your child will be required to take four years of English. At the end of that time your child should be able to:

- Determine the meaning of words and phrases as they are used in a text, including figurative and connotative meanings; analyze the impact of specific word choices on meaning and tone, including words with multiple meanings or language that is particularly fresh, engaging, or beautiful (This should include Shakespeare as well as other authors.);
- Analyze how an author's choices concerning the structure of specific parts of a text (e.g., the choice of where to begin or end a story, the choice to provide a comedic or tragic resolution) contribute to its overall structure and meaning as well as its aesthetic impact;
- Analyze a case in which grasping a point of view requires distinguishing what is directly stated in a text from what is really meant (e.g., satire, sarcasm, irony, or understatement);
- Analyze multiple interpretations of a story, drama, or poem (e.g., recorded or live production of a play or recorded novel or poetry), evaluating how each version interprets the source text (Include at least one play by Shakespeare and one play by an American dramatist.);

- By the end of grade 12, read and comprehend literature of high complexity, including stories, dramas, and poems, independently and proficiently;
- Demonstrate knowledge of eighteenth-, nineteenth- and early-twentieth-century foundational works of American literature, including how two or more texts from the same period treat similar themes or topics.

Math

To graduate, some states only require two upper level math courses, while others require three or four. So if your child took (and passed) Algebra I in eighth grade, all he needs to do to get that diploma might be to take Geometry. But if your child is to be college and career ready, he'll need to do much more than that. Many colleges will expect your child to have completed these courses by the time he enrolls:

8th grade	Algebra I
9th grade	Geometry
10th grade	Algebra II
11th grade	Trigonometry
12th grade	Pre-Calculus or Calculus

The Rest of it

Your child will also need to have firmly established those study skills she's been working on (see Chapter Six for help with that!). And she will have to meet state requirements for social studies/history (often three years, including American History), science (often 2-3 years, including both life and physical sciences), and possibly foreign languages and the arts as well. She must acquire the literacy skills necessary to support the disciplines of interest to her.

How you can nurture this readiness:

Get help from the pros. Just as in middle school, your child's Guidance Counselor can be your best ally in keeping him on track. If your child is headed for college, the Counselor can provide key information such as what classes he will need to meet the requirements of the schools and courses of study that interest him. You'll also want to know how he can prepare both in school and on his own for the standardized testing that will greatly influence his college choices (more on this in Chapter Six). If he's career bound, the counselor can help prepare him for the real world, recommend courses that will support his career interests, and provide information about career options.

So now you have a sense of what's happening for 13 years in that building your child has been building. Yes, it's different from what you and I encountered in ours when we were builders. Join me in Chapter Two for a basic understanding of:

- the new, globally competitive educational goals; and
- how your child's school administrators and teachers measure your child's achievements as she progresses.

Help! I'm Drowning in the Alphabet Sea!

Yes, education administrators have a love affair with the alphabet. After three or four have been lobbed at you in a single sentence, you may feel a little woozy. In fact, so many initials are used in California, where I'm based, that the California Department of Education has a web page devoted to them! Here are a few you might come across frequently (they're all pronounced by saying the initials, unless otherwise indicated):

ACT	American College Testing (a standardized test used for the college admissions process)
AYP	Adequate Yearly Progress (a measure of progress instituted by NCLB, see Chapter Two)
CTT	Collaborative Team Teaching (one Special Ed and one General Ed teacher teaching together in a class of both Special Ed and Gen Ed kids
GLE	Grade Level Expectations (the standards each state sets for kids' learning, grade by grade)
G&T, TAG	(pronounced 'tag') Gifted and Talented Education
or GATE	(pronounced 'gate')
HSEE	High School Exit Exam (each state will have its own groovy name for this one)
IDEA	Individuals with Disabilities Education Act (see Chapter Two)
IEP	Individualized Education Plan (a detailed plan agreed upon by representatives of the DOE and the parents to help your child with physical or developmental issues that interfere with her education)
ESL, EFL	English as a Second Language, English as a Foreign Language
ELL, ESOL	English Language Learners, English for Speakers of Other Languages
NCLB	(pronounced N-C-L-B, or sometimes "nicklebee") No Child Left Behind (see Chapter Two)
SAT	Scholastic Achievement Test (a standardized test used for the college admissions process)
SSR	Sustained Silent Reading (see the box on SSR, above)
SPED	(pronounced 'sped') Special Education

Questions to ask your child's teacher

- What's going on in the classroom? How many teachers are in the classroom? What does a school-day in your classroom look like? In what way does my child work throughout the day?
- What are the grade-level expectations? Is there a chart you can give me showing what my kid needs to master this year to be successful on the end-of-year high stakes assessments (as well as feeling successful and having confidence about her abilities as a student)? What projects/methods are you using to teach these subjects/units?
- What are the problems you face in meeting these goals? i.e., What do you wish you could be doing in class that you just don't have the time for? Are they things that we as parents could be doing at home to help our children master these skills?
- How often are we scheduled to meet with you? How often can we meet if we need to speak more often than that? How would you prefer that we contact you (note in the home folder, email, etc.)? One teacher may love your involvement and want daily contact - another might be annoyed, turn off, and stop responding . . . So asking is key! Email is often best, since it gives the teacher a chance to provide a response at a time when she can reflect with care on your question(s).
- Is there a parent area on the school's website providing information about my child's curriculum, homework, attendance, etc.?
- What type of capability do you have to individualize in the classroom? (I'd be looking to hear that they're giving formative assessments (which I'll define and discuss at length later in the book) and coming up with individualized plans for kids of all levels . . .) How can I support some level of individualization in a large classroom? (At the lower levels, third grade and below, they might need volunteers in the room; in the higher grades, it's more likely to be something you can do at home.)
- How do you determine mastery? How do you determine whether each student is making progress toward mastery? How often throughout the school year do you assess this?

Algebra Across the Grades

In today 's classrooms, kids are asked to begin analytical thinking in each area of study on day one of kindergarten. Related skills and concepts in each area expand and build from year to year. To give you an example of what I mean, I have chosen the areas of study (known as 'domains') relating to Algebra - Operations and Algebraic Thinking for grades K-6, Expressions and Equations for Grades 6-8, and those taught in high school Algebra - and have laid out here the Algebraic skills and concepts for each grade in which they are taught. (Further on, in Chapter Two, I will discuss where these skills and concepts, called 'standards' come from.) As you'll see (and as happens in all subjects, as I wrote above), while "Algebra" is officially taught in ninth grade, its concepts are actually taught with increasing complexity right from the get-go!

Grade K Operations and Algebraic Thinking

- Understand addition as putting together and adding to, and understand subtraction as taking apart and taking from.

  Sample problem: *Indira bought 2 books at the store. Frankie came home from school with 3 books. How many books do they have all together?*

Grade 1 Operations and Algebraic Thinking

- Represent and solve problems involving addition and subtraction.
- Understand and apply properties of operations and the relationship between addition and subtraction.
- Add and subtract within 20.
- Work with addition and subtraction equations.

  Sample Problem: *Indira counted the books in her backpack. She had 5 books. Her friend Frankie counted his as well. Together they have 14 books. How many books does Frankie have?*

Grade 2 Operations and Algebraic Thinking

- Use addition and subtraction within 100 to solve one- and two-step word problems involving situations of adding to, taking from, putting together, taking apart, and comparing, with unknowns in all positions, e.g., by using drawings and equations with a symbol for the unknown number to represent the problem.
- Work with equal groups of objects to gain foundations for multiplication.

  Sample problem: *Indira counted the books she planned to donate to the shelter. She had 29 books. When she added her books to her friend Frankie's, they had 47 books. How many books is Frankie going to donate?*

Grade 3 Operations and Algebraic Thinking

- Represent and solve problems involving multiplication and division.
- Understand properties of multiplication and the relationship between multiplication and division.
- Multiply and divide within 100.
- Solve problems involving the four operations and identify and explain patterns in arithmetic.

  Sample problem: *Frankie and Indira counted the books on the fiction and nonfiction shelves in their classroom at school. Indira counted three times as many books on the fiction shelf as Frankie counted on the nonfiction shelf. Indira counted 136 books. About how many books did Frankie count? If Frankie and Indira are told to divide the books on the two shelves evenly, how many books will there be on each shelf?*

Grade 4 Operations and Algebraic Thinking

- Use the four operations with whole numbers to solve problems.
- Gain familiarity with factors and multiples.
- Generate and analyze patterns.

> Sample problem: *Frankie bought 6 comic books on Sunday. On Monday he returned to the store and bought more comic books. He now has 36 comic books! How many times more comic books did he buy on Monday than on Sunday? If Frankie decides to share the comic books with his 6 friends, how many comic books will each boy get? Write an equation using a variable to represent unknown information.*

Grade 5 Operations and Algebraic Thinking

- Solve word problems involving addition and subtraction of fractions referring to the same whole, including cases of unlike denominators, e.g., by using visual fraction models or equations to represent the problem.
- Use benchmark fractions and number sense of fractions to estimate mentally and assess the reasonableness of answers.
- Solve real world problems involving divisi on of unit fractions by non-zero whole numbers and division of whole numbers by unit fractions, e.g., by using visual fraction models and equations to represent the problem.
- Write and interpret numerical expressions.
- Analyze patterns and relationships.

> Sample problem: *Frankie and Indira visit Books of Wonder Bookstore, which also sells homemade chocolate. Jack buys 7/16 lbs. of chocolate and Sara buys 5/8 lbs. When they get home, they decide to combine their purchases and share the chocolate equally with their little brother Idris. How much chocolate will each person get?*

Grade 6 Expressions and Equations

- Apply and extend previous understandings of arithmetic to algebraic expressions.
- Reason about and solve one-variable equations and inequalities.
- Represent and analyze quantitative relationships between dependent and independent variables.

> Sample problem: *Indira and Frankie take an 80-mile road trip to visit their grandparents. Their mom always drives at a steady rate of 55 miles per hour to stay safe.*
>
> > a. *With mom in the driver's seat, how long will the trip take?*
> > b. *How many miles will the family travel in 18 minutes?*

c. Write an expression for the number of miles they will cover in t minutes of driving.

d. After x minutes of driving, how many miles remain to be covered? Write your answer as a fraction or whole number.

Grade 7 Expressions and Equations

- Use properties of operations to generate equivalent expressions.
- Solve real-life and mathematical problems using numerical and algebraic expressions and equations.

> Sample problem: *Frankie wants to save up enough money so that he can buy a boxed set of books about sports. The complete boxed set costs $60. Frankie has $15 he saved from his birthday. In order to make more money, he plans to wash cars. He plans to charge $6 for each car he washes, and any extra money he makes beyond $60 he can use to buy his sister some books about chess.*
>
> *Write and solve an inequality that represents the number of cars Frankie can wash in order to save at least the minimum amount he needs to buy the boxed set. Graph the solutions on the number line. What is a realistic number of cars for Jonathan to wash? How would that be reflected in the graph?*

Grade 8 Expressions and Equations

- Expressions and Equations Work with radicals and integer exponents.
- Understand the connections between proportional relationships, lines, and linear equations.
- Analyze and solve linear equations and pairs of simultaneous linear equations.

> Sample problem: *Indira and Frankie have a total of 20 books about space exploration between them. After Indira loses three by leaving them on the bus, and some birthday gifts double Frankie's collection, their total increases to 30 books. How many books did each have before these changes? Explain your answer.*

High School Algebra

- Interpret the structure of expressions
- Write expressions in equivalent forms to solve problems
- Perform arithmetic operations on polynomials
- Understand the relationship between zeros and factors of polynomials
- Use polynomial identities to solve problems
- Rewrite rational expressions
- Create equations that describe numbers or relationships
- Understand solving equations as a process of reasoning and explain the reasoning
- Solve equations and inequalities in one variable

- Solve systems of equations
- Represent and solve equations and inequalities graphically

A few sample problems:

Graph this inequality: $y \geq x + 8$

Solve the following simultaneous equations:

$y = x + 8$

$Y = x^2$

Find the point where the equations intersect. $f(x)=5x2 +25x+90 and g(x)=4x 2 +6x+30$

Lorna is planning a surprise party. She is considering using one of two restaurants. Amelia's Kitchen will cost $862 for a reservation, plus $74 per dinner. Brock's Steakhouse will cost $76 per dinner, in-addition to $894 for the reservation. In order to make the best decision, Lorna figures out how many guests it would take to have the venues cost the same amount. What would the total cost be? How many guests would that be?

Not only is today's math different, but the way students are tested in math today is also different from when we were young. And so, it would be worth the time to locate sample test questions on your state's Department of Education website.

CHAPTER TWO

DATA DELIVERS!

You and I have just surveyed the progression of your child's education from kindergarten through high school graduation. Remember the building that is your child's education, with your child as the general contractor? During each year of study, she needs to master the Grade Level Expectations (GLEs, defined in Chapter One) for that grade in all areas of study. These GLEs are the blueprint for that year's floor of the building. Mastering those skills and concepts will create the structural integrity that will support the next level of her skyscraper (the next grade's GLEs) the following year.

How do educators know whether your child has mastered each year's skill set and required knowledge? For that matter, how do they know throughout the year whether the child is progressing adequately in all areas?

They do this through **assessment.** Educational assessment, the process of measuring skills and knowledge, takes many forms and serves many purposes. Everything from class discussion to weekly quizzes to benchmark tests to those big end-of-year standardized tests is a form of assessment. Your child's responses to many forms of assessment are collected as **data.** These data, in sum, give educators information on numerous levels. They illuminate your child's areas of strength and weakness. They measure your child's performance against standards for her grade level, as well as her progress over time. They measure her teachers' effectiveness, and her school's performance in relation to the rest of the country and the world. I will explain assessments and data in greater detail in Chapter Three. But first, let's clarify what I mean by "standards" in the context of education.

Times have changed, and with them, methods of measuring our childrens' performance. Remember filling in all those little circles on testing days? Many kids still have to fill in dots, but whatever the method of testing, the students' answers are measured in a different way now. When we were kids, standardized tests measured our performance against that of other children in our state. As we're about to discuss, academic performance has long been measured against a preset standard. The current trend, however, is to measure each child's performance against his own past performance to assess his growth over time in relation to those standards.

While standards-based teaching and the assessments that go with it have notoriously been used in recent years to compare one school's performance to another for funding purposes, the system was not developed for that reason. It may seem that way, but it really wasn't.

The fact is that standards-based teaching and testing can actually do a lot for your child! They enable schools to identify skill gaps – those areas where your particular child has missed a critical learning objective - and help teachers fill those gaps quickly, before your child falls behind. Furthermore, you may not know this, but under the *Family Educational Rights and Privacy Act* of 1974, you have a legal right to the data collected about your child's performance on these tests, which, as I'll outline in the next chapter, you can use to help your child.

Scope and Sequence: The Substance of the Stuff Your Student is Studying

There's a lot more to your child's lessons than meets the eye. To meet the requirements of its curriculum 'framework,' each district develops a 'Scope and Sequence', or content overview, for all the units to be taught during the year (this is called different things in different districts). The Scope and Sequence is a map from which the teacher can navigate through the year's curriculum. My team and I travel to work with leadership teams in schools in fourteen states on a daily basis. In some districts, the Scope and Sequence is so detailed that a teacher is guided on a day-to-day basis as to what he or she must teach. In others, the Scope and Sequence is greatly determined by textbook choices and content. In still other models, the teacher has more autonomy, as with newer project-based, textbook-free programs. As you can imagine, the success and/or necessity of each of these models is directly related to the talents and experience of the teacher (and leadership of the principal).

Reading for Readiness

While it was commonly known that US students had fallen behind other developed nations in education, it might come as a shock to you to learn that in recent years our students were a full two grade levels behind their foreign counterparts by the time they'd graduate from high school. The creation of Common Core Standards sought to remedy that by drafting standards that bring our graduates to the global table.

The key to this change is a focus on **literacy skills**. Teachers of every subject are expected to incorporate the teaching of literacy skills that relate to the subject area.

Because today's rigorous standards require more complex reading skills across all grade levels and the higher-level thinking that goes along with them, your child is now required to think through every single step in every subject matter in a literate and analytical way. Being able to do so for nonfiction becomes increasingly important as your child reaches higher grades, in preparation for their real-world experiences after graduation.

It is critical, therefore, that your child embraces this process for both fiction and nonfiction. In other words, as I stated in Chapter One and will continue to emphasize throughout this book, *it is critical that you foster in your child not only good reading skills, also a love of reading*. Work with his passions: Find him reading materials on subject that excite him (even if they don't excite you!), and then get in the mix and talk with him about the readings to foster those higher-level thinking skills. For more on this and how to put it into action, see box below, "Depth of Knowledge: Asking the Right Questions."

The Bottom Line for You and Your Child

The bottom line, as I wrote above, is threefold:

1. Because of the adoption of standards and the accumulation of data about student proficiency in those standards, each student's learning profile is carefully mapped throughout her academic career.
2. Under the Family Educational Rights and Privacy Act of 1974, parents have a right to the data collected.
3. This means that you can find out how your child is faring across the board and use what you learn to provide support and reinforcement in the areas in which she is struggling before she falls too far behind.

I will be explaining from here on out how to use data to identify those areas in which your child might need help, how to determine the level of help your child needs, and how to implement an individualized plan for your particular child. Even if your child is already thriving academically, this book can enhance her enjoyment of the learning process and give her tools that will help her succeed not only in school but also throughout her adult life.

If You're Moving

Since many states still use the Common Core State Standards (CCSS), the majority of children will not lose ground in school if they move from one state to another. But for a child moving to or from one of the states that have not adopted the CCSS, small differences in grade level expectations between the two states could make a very large difference.

Devon's parents came to me for help: Devon had lived in California through fourth grade, where he was scheduled to learn to calculate the volume of simple geometric figures in fifth grade. But during the summer between fourth and fifth grades, Devon's family moved to Florida, where students had already covered that material the year before. Devon missed that unit completely, leaving an important structural support out of his Geometry foundation that came back to haunt him when he reached junior high school . . . which was when his parents sought me out. I traced the source of Devon's eighth grade math woes back to what Devon had lost four years earlier because of his interstate move. Most states have adopted Common Core State Standards and other states have created their own based on the new guidelines. Either way, if Devon moved today, it would be much less likely that there would be such a huge gap in his math education.

Since there are several states that do not use CCSS, if you are planning a move out of state, it's a good idea to find out what standards your new state uses and whether they match up with those of your old state so that your child doesn't lose any bricks along the way. If they differ, check out the grade level expectations for the last two grades your child was in for both states, and make sure there won't be any holes. If you see a discrepancy between the standards, you can work at home to help your child catch up and let your child's new teacher know that he might need extra support in a particular area. (Or you might discover that your child is ahead of the game and will have an extra-easy transition - Hoorah!) In Section Three of this book, I will outline the process through which your child can receive extra support both in and out of school should he need it.

If you are moving within your state, there should be little to be concerned about; all the schools in your state are following the same standards. Nevertheless, it's still a good idea to check in with your child's new teacher when you get there, especially if your child is leaving or entering a Special Ed or Gifted and Talented program.

Whether moving in or out of state, I urge you to take the time to have a discussion with your child's new teacher(s), so you can act as a team to support your child with both the academics and social adjustment brought on by the move. I have included suggestions of questions to get you started (see "Questions to Ask Your Child's Teacher," page 31).

"Depth of Knowledge:" Asking the Right Questions

It's no surprise that Educators like to think about thinking. During the 20th century, Thinkers about Thinking began to categorize their thinking into different levels. In the 1950s, Benjamin Bloom headed a committee of educators who introduced the now- famous Bloom's Taxonomy (Don't be alarmed! 'Taxonomy' is just a fancy word for 'categorization'.). Here's what it looks like:

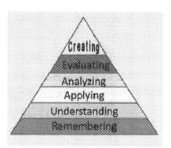

While we were growing up, this way of looking at levels of thinking had a great influence over many theories and methods of teaching. Educators began to consider what kinds of thinking they were asking students to do. This was the beginning of the end of rote memorization as a major focus in education, and a shift towards the goal of teaching young people to think analytically.

Fifty years after Bloom's Taxonomy hit the scene, a somewhat more exacting system of thinking about thought was developed by Norman Webb as a method of aligning assessments with standards. This system is called Webb's Depth of Knowledge. It is not a system of categorization, though, but rather a way of measuring the complexity of thought required by a particular task or question. Here's what that looks like. I am placing a model of DOK (the hip way to refer to Webb's Depth of Knowledge) next to Bloom's, so you can see how the ideas relate:

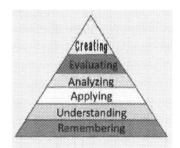

Each of these concepts, of course, is represented in much greater detail by its creator in both written and visual form, but I have set each out in as basic a form as possible here so you can see where this has all led: in a nutshell, educators are encouraging your child to climb those thought pyramids earlier and in more situations than ever before.

Eek, right? It gets better. The two concepts have been combined in recent years as the Cognitive Rigor Matrix, a tool used today by most states to guide curriculum development and lesson planning. I will not print that entire matrix here, because it might make your head spin a bit. But I will show you a simplified version, used in the context of literacy:

The Cognitive Rigor Matrix: Applies Webb's DOK to Bloom's Cognitive Process Dimensions

Depth + thinking	Level 1 Recall & Reproduction	Level 2 Skills & Concepts	Level 3 Strategic Thinking/ Reasoning	Level 4 Extended Thinking
Remember	- Recall, locate basic facts, details, events			
Understand	- Select appropriate words to use when intended meaning is clearly evident	- Specify, explain relationships - summarize - identify main ideas	- Explain, generalize, or connect ideas using supporting evidence (quote, example...)	- Explain how concepts or ideas specifically relate to other content domains or concepts
Apply	- Use language structure (pre/suffix) or word relationships (synonym/antonym) to determine meaning	- Use context to identify meaning of word - Obtain and interpret information using text features	- Use concepts to solve non-routine problems	- Devise an approach among many alternatives to research a novel problem
Analyze	- Identify whether information is contained in a graph, table, etc.	- Compare literary elements, terms, facts, events - analyze format, organization, & text structures	- Analyze or interpret author's craft (literary devices, viewpoint, or potential bias) to critique a text	- Analyze multiple sources - Analyze complex/abstract themes
Evaluate			- Cite evidence and develop a logical argument for conjectures	- Evaluate relevancy, accuracy, & completeness of information
Create	- Brainstorm ideas about a topic	- Generate conjectures based on observations or prior knowledge	- Synthesize information within one source or text	- Synthesize information across multiple sources or texts

Wait, wait, wait, you're saying, what does this mean for lil' ol' me, who spends more time thinking about when-do-I-have-time-to-get-that-oil-change-my-car-needs than thinking about thinking?!

Here's where it matters to you: In keeping with these models and matrices, your child's curriculum is demanding more complex levels of thought from her. Up until recently, teachers asked the vast majority of questions at the lowest levels of DOK, because they needed to show that their students had "mastered the standard," and level 1 and 2 mastery satisfied that requirement. Teachers and students lived at levels 1 and 2 (for the most part). In a recent study, 80% of instruction was happening at DOK 1!

Architects of recently developed educational standards understood that failure of US students to compete in the global marketplace was in large part because we were not asking them to think at higher levels about what they were learning.

We now want our children to apply strategic thinking and reasoning, as well as extended reasoning (see above) to the concepts they are learning, not just recall and reproduce them. This requires a huge shift in how teachers must teach.

And so, your child's teachers are being taught how to ask the kinds of questions that elicit this higher-level thinking, and if you want to best support you child in this, you may wish to learn to ask them, too. Don't panic, it's not hard.

Let's take a few examples:

Your 1st grader loves the book *Don't Let the Pigeon Ride the Bus!* by Mo Willems. (Your 1st grader has great taste - I love that book, too!) Let's think of some questions you could ask after reading the book together:

Who is the main character in this book?

Take a look at the rubric and see where this question would fall. I would place it in the upper left comer, where DOK Level 1 intersects with 'Remember'.

Who is the pigeon talking to and why?

I would place this in Level 2/Understand; the child must understand the concept of the pigeon talking to the reader and must be able to explain why the pigeon addresses the reader.

What do you think the pigeon is going to do next? What makes you say that?

This set of questions requires that the child look for clues about what might happen after the book and cite evidence from the text about her ideas. I would place this at DOK 3/ Understand.

As you can see, young readers will most often not move very far down the rubric (or UP the pyramid!), but it is still possible to ask level 3 and 4 DOK questions, inviting them to think at greater depth about their reading.

Let's think about a text for an older reader. My 6th grade nephew just read The Hunger Games series. Everyone in his class is talking about it. Let's see what kinds of questions we could ask him about his reading . . .

What was The Hunger Games about?

Really, all the child has to do is tell me a plot summary in a coherent way. I'd put this at DOK 1 and at best 'Understand'.

What do think the author's key message is in this series and why?

That's an improvement. I'd put this question at DOK 3/Understand; the child must understand the main message of the book and be able to explain his thinking with evidence from the text.

I think that's about the level of question most of us would be comfortable asking a 6th grader. But what if we want to push him to think a little more in depth and a little more analytically? Let's try stretching him in two ways-I'm going to think of a question that asks him to analyze what the author did, and I'm going to ask him to think across texts:

Hey, you read Divergent, too, right? I noticed a lot of similar themes in those two texts. Do you think the ways the two authors communicated their themes were the same or different? How?

Now that's a stretch question! I'd put that one at DOK 4/Analyze. That's where a 6th grader is going to make some strides in his thinking.

I highly recommend reading with your child and discussing what you've read and pushing yourself to ask the questions that would fall further along the spectrum of deeper, more complex thinking. With an older child, why not start a family book club? There are so many books that are enjoyable at any age. Once you're in heated discussion over Dostoevsky or Verne at the dinner table, you'll realize how much fun it is to spar with your child over books-Boosting his literacy skills will become an enjoyable hobby rather than a chore.

CHAPTER THREE

SUMMATIVE AND FORMATIVE ASSESSMENTS: CRACKING THE CODE

Luis, a bright ten-year old I know, had performed well in math in grades one and two. His mom says he's always been quick with numbers. But in third grade, Luis's grades on math tests went down slightly, and his scores on his end-of year standardized tests in fourth grade were relatively low in math. Luis's parents drilled him with math facts every day at breakfast. That was no biggie - Luis could rattle off his times tables in a snap. His baffled parents considered a math tutor. They couldn't understand why he was struggling when he clearly knew his stuff.

Naya had been an average student in the early grades, but her performance declined in middle school, and now, in high school, she faced the very real possibility that she might not graduate with her classmates. Naya would be devastated to be left behind, but she had no idea how to bring her grades up.

Eighth grader Alex was struggling in all of his subjects and dreaded going to school each day. His parents worried that his struggles would only increase in high school and that they might wind up with a dropout on their hands.

The parents of all three of these children were at a loss. They wanted to help their children but didn't know where to turn. Eventually, each child's parents made their way to me to solve the mystery of their child's academic challenges. And in each instance, I turned to data to crack the case.

What exactly do I mean by "data?" As I mentioned in the previous chapter, data is simply information collected through the various evaluations of your child's learning throughout his academic career. Educators refer to such evaluations as "assessments." These assessments fall into two major categories: Summative and Formative.

Almost anywhere you look, you'll see the following explanation of the distinction between these two types of assessments: Summative assessments are assessments *of* learning; Formative assessments are assessments *for* learning.

Helpful, right? Not necessarily, at least not until you already know the distinction. So to help parents understand which is which, I sometimes describe it this way:

Summative assessments are assessments that **sum up** your child's knowledge and skills at a particular moment in time; **Formative** assessments are used to help **formulate** the next step of your child's learning path.

To explain what I mean and to see how the two forms of assessments can be helpful to you, let's delve into each one:

<u>Summative Assessments:</u>

A Summative assessment is like a snapshot of your child's knowledge and/or skills at a particular point in time. Summative assessments take many forms, from an end-of-the- week spelling test to formal statewide testing. Some of the summative tests you may have seen your child bring home from school are:

- end-of-unit or end-of-chapter tests;
- midterm exams;
- final projects;
- final exams.

These and other types of summative assessments often contribute toward your child's mid-year or final grade in a subject.

The summative assessments that tend to strike the most fear in everyone's hearts are those big standardized statewide tests that determine a school's rank or grade as well as the funding it receives. The reason these Scare the dickens out of the students who take them and their parents too, -is that these tests also often determine acceptance into a good middle school, high school or college. The ultimate standardized test for college- bound students is the Scholastic Aptitude Test (SAT) and American College Testing exam (ACT).

They may be scary, but they serve a particular purpose. Summative Assessments are not given during the learning process to help teachers figure out how effectively they are teaching. Rather, Summative Assessments are given after the fact - at the end of a unit, a semester, or a whole school year - to assess whether their students have mastered a particular set of skills and knowledge. Summative Assessments thus create accountability on several levels:

- **Students** are held accountable when taking such Summative Assessments as midterms and final exams by being given grades in the subject areas tested. Standardized tests may also determine whether a student gets into a middle school, high school or college of her choice.
- **Teachers** are held accountable for their performance in the classroom (for purposes of continued employment, seniority and tenure) based in part upon their students' scores on standardized tests.
- **Schools, districts and states** are held accountable for their effectiveness in educating their students through the allocation of state and federal funds based on their students' performance on standardized tests.

Right now, you're probably thinking, "What does this have to do with the price of lunch boxes in Poughkeepsie?" Although districts and states gather summative data to evaluate school performance and qualify for funding, this data can actually be very useful to you! As I mentioned in Chapter Two, you have a legal right to this data. (To learn how to get this data, see "Getting Your Mitts on Those Summative Assessment Scores" Box, page 57) As you're about to see, a careful look at your child's test scores can reveal his areas of strength and weakness and will point you towards the right plan of action. Remember Luis, Naya and Alex? I sat with their parents and helped them go through just such a process. Let's look at what I discovered about each child in turn.

Luis, as you recall, was suddenly falling behind in math, despite knowing his math facts and understanding the concepts inside and out. An examination of his fourth grade year-end standardized test results revealed that math facts and concepts were not, in fact, the problem. I saw the culprit right away - it was as plain as the giant "Go Speed Racer!" logo emblazoned across his T-shirt!

I looked at Luis's math scores. As you can see from this snapshot of his summative assessment, this former math whiz was losing ground. But the dots on the math side of the page were not the ones that caught my eye.

Rather, it was a solitary little dot in the English Language Arts (ELA) column across from the words, "Reading Comprehension."

Your child's strengths and needs based on these tests

A NOTE ON USING THIS INFORMATION: A single test can provide only limited information. A student taking the same test more than once might score higher or lower in each tested area within a small range. You should confirm your child's strengths and needs in these topics by reviewing classroom work, standards-based assessments, and your child's progress reports during the year.

Find released test items at **www.cde.ca.gov/ta/ tg/sr/resources.asp** and a complete copy of the standards at **www.cde.ca.gov/be/st/ss**.

* In the charts below, your child's percent correct is compared to the percent correct of students statewide whose performance level was Proficient. Proficient is the state target for all students.

English-Language Arts   GRADE 4

Content Areas	Your Child's #	Your Child's %	Your Child's Percent Correct (♦) Compared to the Percent Correct Range of Proficient Students (—)
Reading			0% 25% 50% 75% 100%
Word Analysis and Vocabulary Development	14	78%	
Reading Comprehension	6	40%	
Literary Response and Analysis	3	33%	
Writing			
Written Conventions	11	61%	
Writing Strategies	8	53%	
Writing Applications Score		50%	

= Number of Correct Items   % = Percent Correct

Mathematics   GRADE 4

Content Areas	Your Child's #	Your Child's %	Your Child's Percent Correct (♦) Compared to the Percent Correct Range of Proficient Students (—)
Decimals, Fractions, and Negative Numbers	12	71%	0% 25% 50% 75% 100%
Operations and Factoring	9	64%	
Algebra and Functions	14	78%	
Measurement and Geometry	8	67%	
Statistics, Data Analysis, and Probability	0	0%	

More about the English-Language Arts Standards

Word Analysis, Fluency, and Systematic Vocabulary Development: Students understand the basic features of reading. They select letter patterns and know how to translate them into spoken language by using phonics, syllabication, and word parts. They apply this knowledge to achieve fluent oral and silent reading.

Reading Comprehension: Students read and understand grade-level-appropriate material. They draw upon a variety of comprehension strategies as needed (e.g., generating and responding to essential questions, making predictions, comparing information from several sources).

Literary Response and Analysis: Students read and respond to a wide variety of significant works of children's literature. They distinguish between the structural features of the text and the literary terms or elements (e.g., theme, plot, setting, characters).

Written Conventions: Students write and speak with a command of standard English conventions appropriate to this grade level.

Writing Strategies: Students write clear, coherent sentences and paragraphs that develop a central idea. Their writing shows they consider the audience and purpose. Students progress through the stages of the writing process (e.g., prewriting, drafting, revising, editing successive versions).

Writing Applications: Students write compositions that describe and explain familiar objects, events, and experiences.

More about the Mathematics Standards

Number Sense: Students understand the place value of whole numbers and decimals to two decimal places and how whole numbers and decimals relate to simple fractions. Students use the concepts of negative numbers. Students extend their use and understanding of whole numbers to the addition and subtraction of simple decimals. Students solve problems involving addition, subtraction, multiplication, and division of whole numbers and understand the relationships among the operations. Students know how to factor small whole numbers.

Algebra and Functions: Students use and interpret variables, mathematical symbols, and properties to write and simplify expressions and sentences. Students know how to manipulate equations.

Measurement and Geometry: Students understand perimeter and area. Students use two-dimensional coordinate grids to represent points and graph lines and simple figures. Students demonstrate an understanding of plane and solid geometric objects and use this knowledge to show relationships and solve problems.

Statistics, Data Analysis, and Probability: Students organize, represent, and interpret numerical and categorical data and clearly communicate their findings. Students make predictions for simple probability situations.

As you can see, Luis scored pretty well in his other ELA subjects, or "strands." But he was having trouble with reading comprehension. Wouldn'tcha know - third grade (which, as you'll recall, is when Luis began slipping in math) is the first year in which a great emphasis in math is placed on word problems, and by fourth grade, word problems are even more complex. Luis wasn't having a problem with his math facts; his math challenges were actually *reading challenges*.

When I asked Luis what books he liked to read, I was not surprised to hear that reading has never been his favorite activity, to put it mildly. But why might he not love to read? His scores provided good clues. If you take a look at Luis's ELA scores, you will notice that his 74th percentile score in vocab is bringing up his average score. The reality is that all his other scores in ELA are alarmingly low: 26th percentile in Reading Comprehension, 23rdpercentile in Literary Response and Analysis, 25th percentile in in Written Conventions, and 17th percentile in Writing Applications.

All of this points in one direction: while Luis was accumulating a great English vocabulary, he was losing ground in reading comprehension and in his writing skills (students' writing scores are always a little bit lower than their reading scores, since the written response is dependent on having understood what they've read). So, to answer my own question, why might Luis not love to read? Because it was difficult for him, and what kid likes to do something that feels like a chore? And, as I've said before, a child not only needs to be able to read, but to love to read, in order to succeed in all areas of school.

You might then ask why his family had not flagged the English as a challenge. Why just the math? Well, for Luis and his family, English was a second language, and so his family chalked his difficulties up to that fact. They knew reading was a challenge and he was already getting additional assistance in English, so his parents assumed that he was well on his way to improving in this subject area. As it turns out, though, the two days per week of additional small group instruction he was receiving were not enough to remediate his challenges. Luis needed more.

A math tutor would have been a big waste of his parents' money and his time. It turned out Luis needed more help from his school. I helped his parents explain to his principal and teacher that he should be switched into the next level of reading support at school (in Chapter Ten, I will explain the tiered system of academic support that is now standard in schools), which in Luis's case meant he would come to school a half hour early every day for an online reading intervention program in the school library with an aide. The school agreed, and, furthermore, Luis received ongoing progress monitoring every two weeks.

As for the home component of the plan, I made recommendations that addressed word problems in math and reading comprehension: I first suggested that Luis's parents add an online math program to his homework regimen three times per week for twenty minutes, tailored around the word problems. This proved too expensive for the family, so I recommended Khan Academy, an excellent free online resource, instead. Since Luis's family does not have access to the Internet at home, Luis's father asked the school for permission to use computers in the school's library after school hours, which the principal was happy to grant. And Luis happily used the local library 's computers on weekends – he was permitted an extra half-hour of screen-time to play video games after completing his reading assignment each visit. I asked that Luis's parents focus Luis's efforts on word problems. And since Luis loves sports, I asked his father to please have him read articles from the local newspaper and then summarize the content and answer his father's questions about it. Here are some sample questions I suggested to Luis's father:

- What was the article about?
- Who were the people featured in it, and what did they do?
- What was your opinion before you read the article, and did reading the article change that opinion?
- What specifically did you read that changed your mind?

And as I explained to Luis's parents, he could even be reading these articles and discussing them in his native Spanish - reading comprehension is reading comprehension, whatever the language. Remember - Luis didn't need help with English decoding or vocabulary.

That fall, we held a conference call with Luis's new fifth grade teacher, who agreed to slip in some extra comprehension work during vocab and spelling periods, since he was already strong in those areas.

This example highlights the importance of properly diagnosing your child's areas of challenge. Remember the construction site metaphor I used at the top of Chapter One? We can see clearly how weak skills in one area hamper success (especially when the weak area is literacy). That scenario will only intensify over time. A child cannot build the fourth or fifth floor of her educational building when some of the third floor's beams are not sound.

Luis's parents and I were able to discover the root of his backslide in math, . . . and interpretation of data led us to a few easy fixes that soon had him speeding through those word problems like Speed Racer in his trusty Mach 5.

Word Problems? Not a Problem!

The one constant you may have noticed in this book, all the way from kindergarten through high school, is my emphasis on literacy. That's because most of the ground we're exploring together is heavily influenced by the newer, more universal standards, which focus on literacy across all the subjects. Educator are now expected – and required – to bring literacy into *every* subject they teach – and yes, that includes math! So if there is one single thing you can do that will give your child a boost throughout his school day, including during math class, it's ensuring that his literacy skills are constantly improving.

My young friend Naya, whom you also met above, is bubbly, funny and kind-hearted - traits that have carried her far in her school career. A popular girl, she is adored by her friends. Teachers like her too, as she often makes valuable contributions to class discussions. But her teachers were also concerned about her, not to mention surprised, because her written work and exams were not reflecting the high level thinking she had demonstrated in class. As you will soon see from her standardized test results, she performed at the "Far Below Basic" Level in most of her eleventh-grade subject areas.

As a result, as I mentioned at the top of this chapter, Naya was very afraid that she would not be graduating with her friends the next year.

I gleaned a bit more background about Naya from her mom when she first came to me for help: Naya had been an okay student in elementary school, performing in the average range for her grade each year. While her grades slipped a bit in fifth grade, this raised no flags, since her test scores were still in the "proficient" range.

In sixth grade, however, the academic and organizational demands on Naya increased, and her performance decreased. Throughout middle school, Naya's grades, test scores and self-esteem gradually declined.

And in high school, they bottomed out.

I had a good hunch about what was going on. Speaking with Naya herself increased my suspicions. Naya confided in me that her world was rocked in sixth grade when her parents divorced. She hadn't seen it coming. And to make matters worse, her parents' separation was a very acrimonious one, in which the two fought loudly and continuously and tried to pit Naya against one another. No wonder her mother hadn't mentioned anything about it to me.

Two things about this: First of all, the stress on Naya directly impacted her ability to concentrate and perform in school, right at sixth grade, when schools expect greater independence and organizational abilities, and when academic demands increase greatly. Second, everyone was so busy with the divorce that no one noticed Naya's mounting academic struggles or interceded to support her (more on the effects of various stressors on academic success in Chapter Nine).

Naya's mother was struggling financially, and in time, she and Naya moved in with Naya's grandmother, reestablishing some stability in Naya's home life by eighth grade.

Meanwhile, how did her parents' divorce fit in with Naya's larger academic picture? And why didn't her grades improve once she was living with her grandmother?

I turned to Naya's standardized test scores, and sure enough, they instantly confirmed my initial suspicions. What leapt off the page at me were those few diamonds that fell above the 50th percentile, which reflected markedly higher scores than any of the other scores. What did these outlier scores all have in common?.

Your child's strengths and needs based on these tests

A NOTE ON USING THIS INFORMATION: A single test can provide only limited information. A student taking the same test more than once might score higher or lower in each tested area within a small range. You should confirm your child's strengths and needs in these topics by reviewing classroom work, standards-based assessments, and your child's progress reports during the year.

Find released test items at **www.cde.ca.gov/ta/tg/sr/resources.asp** and a complete copy of the standards at **www.cde.ca.gov/be/st/ss**.

In the charts below, your child's percent correct is compared to the percent correct range of students statewide whose performance level was Proficient on the total test. Proficient is the state target for all students.

English-Language Arts   GRADE 11

Content Areas	#	%	Your Child's Percent Correct (♦) Compared to the Percent Correct Range of Proficient Students (▬)
Reading			
Word Analysis and Vocabulary Development	3	38%	
Reading Comprehension	5	26%	
Literary Response and Analysis	9	53%	
Writing			
Written Conventions	2	22%	
Writing Strategies	5	23%	

= Number of Correct Items   % = Percent Correct

Mathematics

Content Areas	#	%	Your Child's Percent Correct (♦) Compared to the Percent Correct Range of Proficient Students (▬)

Your child did not take a California Standards Test in this subject.

World History

Content Areas	#	%	Your Child's Percent Correct (♦) Compared to the Percent Correct Range of Proficient Students (▬)

Your child did not take a California Standards Test in this subject.

Chemistry

Content Areas	#	%	Your Child's Percent Correct (♦) Compared to the Percent Correct Range of Proficient Students (▬)
Atomic and Molecular Structure	3	38%	
Chemical Bonds, Biochemistry	6	67%	
Kinetics, Thermodynamics	2	14%	
Chemical Reactions	4	31%	
Conservation of Matter and Stoichiometry	1	10%	
Investigation and Experimentation	4	67%	

California Reading List (CRL)

Your child's recommended California Reading List Number is 8.

This recommended reading list number is based on your child's California English-Language Arts Standards Test score. While the CRL will provide you with a list of titles, no single score will tell you what books your child can or should read - encourage your child to explore other reading list numbers to find books of interest.

To access the California Reading List:
- Visit **http://star.cde.ca.gov** and click on California Reading List
- Click Search for a Reading List to find books for your child

Early Assessment Program (EAP)

English Status: Not yet demonstrating readiness for CSU college-level English courses
Mathematics Status: Not Applicable

EAP statuses are provided by the CSU. Explanation of EAP statuses

U.S. History   GRADE 11

Content Areas	#	%	Your Child's Percent Correct (♦) Compared to the Percent Correct Range of Proficient Students (▬)
Foundations of Amer. Pol. & Social Thought	3	30%	
Industrialization and the U.S. Role as a World Power	5	38%	
United States Between the World Wars	4	33%	
World War II and Foreign Affairs	3	25%	
Post-World War II Domestic Issues	1	8%	

Well, they were all in subject areas that require higher-level analytical thinking and very little reading comprehension and fact gathering. The scores made perfect sense for the girl with good ideas in class, where she was listening intently and applying her smarts. . .*but who had never developed the study skills required to keep her literacy skills at grade level as demands increased.*

Without those study and literacy skills, it was impossible for Naya to keep up with any of her subjects once she reached high school, where the work is challenging, and there's lots of it. Academic losses are cumulative - subjects taught each year build on the acquired knowledge and skills of the previous year. Naya found herself in a bigger and bigger ditch that was harder and harder to climb out of, and by eleventh grade was simply faking it as best she could. And so, in each subject, she would deliver well enough in class but flounder in her homework and on exams.

Naya's cheery disposition, popularity, and desire to participate in class (where she could feel her most competent) helped her do a great job of faking her way through her academic career, until the demands caught up with her and made it impossible to continue. Today, schools have protections in place at every grade level that - had they existed when Naya was younger - theoretically would have helped set Naya on the right path far earlier (I'll discuss this protocol - called RTI - further in Chapter Ten). For Naya' s mother and educators, however, there was no single place to turn for an understanding of the Big Picture except her standardized test results. The data in those reports painted a vivid picture of her situation that led to her finally catching up on the study and homework skills she needed to succeed in school and graduate on time. She did it! In the section of this book I've entitled, "Your Child's Best Self," I'll help you understand your child's learning style and guide you as you instill great study and homework skills in your child, too.

And as for Alex, as soon as I saw his sullen face when his mom brought him to see me, I knew he was miserably unhappy. This poor middle-schooler was still struggling with schoolwork despite a progression of tutors, as well as extra help in class, during school, before school and after school. A review of notes and reports from teachers, tutors and guidance counselor revealed a young teen who hated going to school, hated his parents and teachers for making him go, and hated himself for his repeated failures.

As you can see, Alex's standardized test results for seventh and eighth grades show a child performing below the proficiency range in scores for all subjects save one eighth- grade math content area (that for rational numbers).

Your child's strengths and needs based on these tests

A NOTE ON USING THIS INFORMATION: A single test can provide only limited information. A student taking the same test more than once might score higher or lower in each tested area within a small range. You should confirm your child's strengths and needs in these topics by reviewing classroom work, standards-based assessments, and your child's progress reports during the year.

Find released test items at **www.cde.ca.gov/ta/tg/sr/resources.asp** and a complete copy of the standards at **www.cde.ca.gov/be/st/ss**.

In the charts below, your child's percent correct is compared to the percent correct range of students statewide whose performance level was Proficient on the total test. Proficient is the state target for all students.

English-Language Arts   GRADE 8

Content Areas	#	%	Your Child's Percent Correct (♦) Compared to the Percent Correct Range of Proficient Students (━)
Reading			
Word Analysis and Vocabulary Development	5	56%	
Reading Comprehension	10	56%	
Literary Response and Analysis	6	40%	
Writing			
Written Conventions	4	25%	
Writing Strategies	5	29%	

= Number of Correct Items   % = Percent Correct

General Mathematics

Content Areas	#	%	Your Child's Percent Correct (♦) Compared to the Percent Correct Range of Proficient Students (━)
Rational Numbers	10	71%	
Exponents, Powers, and Roots	5	50%	
Quant. Relationships and Evaluating Expressions	2	18%	
Multistep Problems, Graphing, and Functions	2	20%	
Measurement and Geometry	2	18%	
Statistics, Data Analysis, and Probability	4	44%	

History-Social Science   GRADE 8

Content Areas	#	%	Your Child's Percent Correct (♦) Compared to the Percent Correct Range of Proficient Students (━)
World History and Geography: Ancient Civ.	9	56%	
Late Antiquity and the Middle Ages	6	43%	
Renaissance/Reformation	4	40%	
U.S. Constitution and the Early Republic	12	55%	
Civil War and its Aftermath	8	62%	

Science   GRADE 8

Content Areas	#	%	Your Child's Percent Correct (♦) Compared to the Percent Correct Range of Proficient Students (━)
Motion	1	13%	
Forces, Density, and Buoyancy	7	54%	
Structure of Matter and Periodic Table	7	44%	
Earth in the Solar System	2	29%	
Reactions and the Chemistry of Living Systems	5	50%	
Investigation and Experimentation	2	33%	

I could not help but wonder why Alex had not yet been referred for screening to pinpoint learning challenges. I wondered this aloud and told his mother how she and Alex's dad could launch the process (I'll discuss this further in Section Three of this book). Alex needed greater support than he had been receiving from tutors and even from in-school and after-school resource centers. His screening revealed two specific learning differences for which Alex received the necessary accommodations and treatment. I am very relieved and happy to report to you that Alex is now getting better grades. More important, he no longer dreads school. When I saw him for a recent follow-up meeting, I saw a more relaxed and comfortable young man. It turns out that Alex has a beautiful smile.

Getting Your Mitts on Those Summative Assessment Scores

Every state's Department of Education has a website where the state's summative test scores are stored. If your school has not already given you your child's particular UserID and Password, you would need to ask your child's teacher or principal for them, so that you may access that information.

So now you can see why it is said that Summative Assessments *sum up* learning (and how that info, while useful to districts, the state and the feds, can also be useful to YOU!). Now I'll explain what Formative Assessments are, and you'll quickly understand why they are explained as *being/or* learning, i.e., in order to *formulate* each child's learning path as the child goes.

> **Summative** assessments are assessments that **sum up** your child's knowledge and skills at a particular moment in time; **Formative** assessments are used to help **formulate** the next step of your child's learning path.

Formative Assessments:

OK, so now we're clear that Summative Assessments measure a student's mastery of skills and concepts *after the fact,* to create accountability. Formative Assessments, on the other hand, measure each student's understanding of skills and concepts *as the learning occurs;* in response, the teacher then modifies his teaching to each child's individual needs as those needs change throughout the school year.

Formative Assessments take many shapes and can even look exactly like Summative Assessments. In fact, the same assessment can sometimes be used for either purpose. Really? Yes - the difference lies in how the results are used. While they may yield scores, Formative Assessments are not used for grading; rather, they provide the feedback teachers need to adapt their teaching, so that they can make that teaching as targeted as possible. What defines a Formative Assessment is simply the fact that it is used to guide teaching.

You may not realize it (and your child surely doesn't, either!), but in addition to two to four periodic formative tests per year (which we'll discuss further, below), Formative Assessments are taking place in big and small ways in the classroom every day of the school year. There are almost as many types of Formative Assessments as there are teachers to give them.

Here is a sampling of the types of Formative Assessments being used in your child's classroom on an ongoing basis. Variations of these types of Formative Assessments are used throughout grades K-12. Remember that your kid probably has no idea that his progress is being assessed:

- Class discussions, during which the teacher is observing the students' responses and often recording them;
- Essays demonstrating mastery of content in a particular subject, or mastery of particular writing skills at the child's current level;
- Pop quizzes given to assess a child's mastery of the current content being taught;
- Group activities in which the teacher poses a mathematical problem that has more than one solution. Kids work together to compare ideas and understand how their different mathematical ideas are related. The teacher carefully monitors the thought processes of the students, noting each child's strengths and weaknesses in mathematical thinking (This

type of assessment is referred to by educators as a Generative Activity, in case you wanted to impress the teacher.);

- Group activities in which a teacher asks students to solve a real-life problem that naturally leads towards the concepts he hopes to teach. The goal is for the students to find their own path to discovering the mathematical model by sharing ideas and trying them out. The teacher listens to and observes the students' thinking and strategies (This type of assessment is called a Model-eliciting Activity.);
- Lab reports used to elicit a child's understanding of the science behind the experiment;
- Self-assessments in many forms, ranging from a simple one-page checklist for kids to fill out post-unit to hand-signals used by kids in the classroom to indicate how well they are following a lesson;
- Portfolios of student work, updated regularly, as records of individual progress in relation to the standards and to each child's particular challenges.

Teaching Teamwork While Testing

One of the reasons that group activities are used so often in classrooms is to foster collaborative skills. The ability to work well with others is an important key to success in the working world, and the earlier students begin honing this ability, the better equipped they will be once they're out there.

All of the above are used for all grade levels, though more so - and with increasing complexity - as the child progresses through the grades. If your child is still in elementary school, here are a few key Formative Assessments that are employed more regularly in those early grades, when those critical literacy and math foundations are being developed:

READING

Individual reading assessments are used to find each child's "just-right" level. Each student is tested regularly throughout the year, usually by reading aloud a preselected passage while the teacher measures the child's ability to read fluently, decode difficult words, and understand content; the child is then assigned a reading level that is appropriate for her, with just the right amount of challenge (for more on the idea and importance of "just right" reading, see "Leveled Reading: State of the Art Reading for Elementary School" in Chapter One, page 20.)

WRITING

Writing is often assessed in student conference, one-on-one with the teacher. The teacher sits with the child and reviews the current piece of writing to see whether he 'got' that day's lesson; the teacher also checks over the writing for skills the child is working to master. For instance, she may remind one child that we capitalize proper nouns, then move on to encourage the next child to include more dialogue or descriptive words, and then help a third understand what makes a complete sentence.

Writing with Rubrics

Rubrics - assessment tools for student performance - are embedded right into the instructional process for teaching students to write clearly, and with correct grammar, solid structure, progression of logic and purpose. Your young writer should regularly receive rubrics from her teacher to use as a guideline when completing writing assignments. Taping the rubric up where your child is working at home can help your child double-check her work against the rubric to be sure she has covered all her bases.

MATH

In schools where it is possible to create small-group math instruction, pre-unit tests are used to continuously sort students into groups according to specific skills and knowledge.

In a perfect world, teachers would have the time and resources to figure out exactly what these Formative Assessments are saying about each child, in a nuanced and detailed way. In reality, large class sizes and increasing demands with regard to the curricula to be covered can prevent even the most talented teachers from assessing exactly where a particular child's trouble spot originates.

When my neighbor's daughter began slipping in geometry, a glance at her last five pop quizzes and a discussion with the tenth grader revealed that she didn't understand the use of letters to designate parts of a triangle.

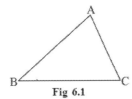

Fig 6.1

This is so obvious to most people that it hadn't even been explained to her class by her teacher. But, as her mom told me later, her teacher reviewed these formative assessments, got a hunch about what was going on, and confirmed it with a ten-minute conversation . . . and the issue was resolved before she fell too far behind to regain her footing. This wasn't even a math issue; it was a failure to understand a convention.

As **a parent, what can you do?** Show an interest in your child's week-by-week learning. This happens in a few ways: through conversation with your child and with her teacher, and by looking at your child's work. Your child may be reluctant to share her work with you. Show that you're taking an interest anyway, but, depending on your child's age, don't push her to share. You can get the answers you need from her teacher(s).

Teachers sit up and pay attention when they see that a child's parents are doing the same. It is always a good idea to be in touch with your child's teachers at the beginning of the school year, to introduce yourself, and to let them know that you are eager to support their classroom efforts at home. Further, you should respectfully request that should their ongoing formative assessments begin to suggest that your child is challenged by a new concept or skill, you would greatly appreciate it if they would let you know right away . . . again, so that you can support their efforts and help get your child back on track.

> Teachers sit up and pay attention when they see that a child's parents are doing the same.

If you're ready to help your child in ways from small to big, you can jump right in by heading on over to Section Two. But for those History Wonks among you, I'm wrapping up this section about schooling in the US with a brief overview of how public education in our country has evolved in recent history.

Lexile Reading Levels for Life-Readiness

My friend's daughter goes to a small school that has a school-wide reading hour every morning. The children are grouped with others who read at their level, and for that one hour of each day, the children leave their regular classrooms (where their classmates are at varying reading levels) and go to their reading groups for their literacy studies. I love this school!

"But how does the school know the children's precise reading levels?" All U.S. elementary schools now periodically assess every child's reading level. There are many systems used, but Lexile, which I'm about to describe below, is the most common one. For the most part, these systems use the same types of methods for assessment. Each child is tested using a "benchmark" text at the beginning of the school year, is placed at the appropriate level, and is retested regularly throughout the school year to determine whether he is ready to move ahead. If your child regularly brings home books from school labeled with a letter or a number, it relates to the leveling system his school uses.

And it's not only the student who is assessed. Books and other reading materials are also assessed for their difficulty, and their levels determined. Students can then be assigned reading material that is at the "just right" level for them (hence teachers urging parents to have their children reading at their "just right" levels).

Your child's reading level is most likely measured in another way, as well. Along with the results of yearly summative testing or yearly administration of the Scholastic Reading Inventory (you got it, SRI!) test, you most likely receive another measure of your child's reading level, known as his "Lexile Level." The Lexile system is the one almost exclusively used by administrators and school systems to evaluate the success of schools, school districts, literacy programs, etc. It is also used by the Common Core State Standards to cite specific text levels within standards. In other words, it is by way of your child's Lexile Measure that he will be assessed in relation to his Grade Level Expectations.

"So why doesn't my child's school just use the Lexile Level as his reading level?" Great question. That's because the Lexile Measure only takes into account a text's level based on factors such as word usage and sentence complexity. Even Common Core recommends that schools use other systems when actually matching up students and books. Systems used in schools take into account many additional factors, such as interest level, content and theme appropriateness, and multiple levels of meaning. These systems also provide simple, standard ways for teachers to assess children on a regular basis.

"What does that mean for me, as a parent?" First, it means that you will want to find books at your child's level that entice him to read. You can go directly to Lexile.com online. Another common resource for both schools and parent for children's books is Scholastic, which provides a wonderful resource online in its Teacher Book Wizard.

This section of the Scholastic website allows teachers and parents to find out the Lexile Level of hundreds of books. Either way, you can search for books within particular reading levels, genres, ages, and interests. Don't worry if you can 't find a level within your school's system. Often books at the library, bookstore or even listed in the Teacher Book Wizard are only measured according to one or two of the many systems. That's ok. There are many book-leveling conversion charts available to help you get very close to a book's level within your child's particular system. (See Appendix E for a chart that gives approximate conversions for several systems.)

The Later Years – Lexile Levels for Living Life

As your child moves on to middle school and beyond, he will no longer be assessed the leveling systems. . .But his Lexile Level will probably still be measured yearly. The periodic assessment of reading levels ends because your child is now reading "adult literature," which is beyond the scope of the systems used in elementary school. But don't be fooled-your child 's actual literacy skills are (or should be!) continuing to improve, and that improvement is very important! Because there's something else I want you to know about Lexile levels:

Although surveys have shown that 95% of eighth-graders in the US aspire to go to college, only 37% of high school graduates were actually prepared to succeed in college, as measured by their Lexile level. This is precisely what Common Core sought to correct.

Furthermore, our young people were not graduating high school at high enough Lexile levels to be competitive in the work force, never mind in the global marketplace. In fact, their Lexile levels were not even high enough to comprehend a simple instruction booklet for installing a new baby's car seat! No joke ... and not funny.

When Common Core was first implemented, graduates averaged a Lexile level of 960. But the materials that a person will encounter and have to comprehend and evaluate in his first job after high school start at Lexile levels of approximately 1100 at the very lowest. Uh-oh.

And so Common Core sought to raise the Lexile levels of our high school graduates by what amounts to approximately two full grade-levels across the nation.

Here is a chart of the average range of Lexile levels by grade.

Grade	College & Career Ready Lexile Bands
1	190L to 530L
2	420L to 650L
3	520L to 820L
4	740L to 940L
5	830L to 1010L
6	925L to 1070L
7	970L to 1120L
8	1010L to 1185L
9	1050L to 1260L
10	1080L to 1335L
11 and 12	1185L to 1385L

And here is a chart of the Lexile levels needed to read particular everyday materials:

Everyday Reading Materials	Lexile (L)
Job Application	1060L
College Application	1160L
Bank Statement	1200L
New York Times Article/Daily News	1490L
Ford Escape Owner's Manual	1190L
Apartment Lease Agreement	1300L
Medical Brochure – Type 2 Diabetes	970L

Reading Skills and the Career Readiness Gap. International Center for Leadership in Education. July 2014. Successful Practices Network. Appendix B.

And here is a graph of the Lexile levels needed to hold particular jobs:

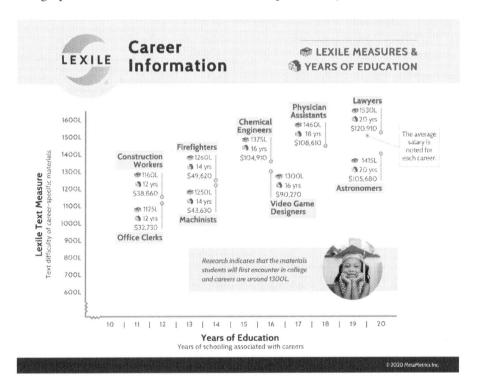

You're reading this book. You're taking an active interest in your child's literacy and education. You're making a difference. By helping her read well – and enjoy doing so – you're helping her achieve, not only now in school, but in the future in her career … and in her life.

CHAPTER FOUR

FOR HISTORY WONKS

I know, I know - not everyone is an education-geek like I am, but I have had so many parents asking why their children's educational experience is so different than their own had been, and since almost none of those parents' eyes glazed over when I explained the progression of public education in the US, I think it's worth setting it out here for you. So, history buffs, read on! But if you want to jump straight into how to help your child succeed in school, my inner nerd's feelings will not be hurt if you skip this chapter.

B.C.C. (Before Common Core)

For decades, the U.S. government has been trying to narrow the "achievement gap" between students of different socioeconomic backgrounds in the U.S. More recently, it has also tried to address the alarming statistics that indicate that our students have fallen behind their peers in other first-world nations.

In 1965, President Lyndon B. Johnson signed into law the Elementary and Secondary Education Act (ESEA), legislation originally proposed by his predecessor, John F. Kennedy. ESEA was the cornerstone of Johnson's "War on Poverty." It marked the first time that the federal government became involved in what had previously been the domain of states and municipalities.

The next major development came with the No Child Left Behind Act of 2001 (NCLB), proposed by George W. Bush. NCLB introduced standards-based education reform, which deeply affected public school education in the U.S., because for the first time, public school funding was tied to student performance.

The No Child Left Behind Act (NCLB) of 2002 moved us from "norm-referenced testing", which compares kids to a sampling of other kids on a broad range of skills (and which doesn't measure student knowledge of a specific curriculum) to "criterion referenced" testing, which makes very specific standards-based comparisons (and which does measure understanding of specific content). Although it did not establish national standards, NCLB mandated that each state follow *some* set of standards. Since NCLB funding is tied to the adoption of standards and to students meeting a level of proficiency in those standards, it has had a large impact.

Because of the funding link, NCLB did have the desired effect of inducing all states to implement some educational standards and to test their children against those standards. But NCLB emphasized extra supports for children with learning differences, with the unwanted effect of failing to help children early enough to avoid the need for drastic interventions. Further, it has had an ironic result - the reduction in funding for the very schools that need it the most. And many detractors of NCLB also feel it has caused educators to "teach to the test," thereby limiting the subjects that can be taught and the level of students' abstract thinking, as well as limiting teacher creativity.

CCE (Common Core Era): Understanding Standards

Soon after he stepped into office, President Barack Obama launched a multi-pronged initiative to address the failings of NCLB and the ongoing shortcomings in US education in relation to that of other first-world nations. Shifting the focus of education to *ensuring college and career readiness in the global market,* President Obama pushed for educational "standards and assessments that don't simply measure whether students can fill in a bubble on a test, but whether they possess 21st century skills like problem solving and critical thinking and entrepreneurship and creativity."

The Obama Administration then issued an extensive blueprint for NCLB's reform Included in this plan is a requirement for all states to adjust their standards to "build toward college and career readiness".

What do I mean by this? Historically, each state would gather panels and teams of curriculum experts to develop its own standards, which the Board of Education (BOE) of that state would debate (usually encouraging parental and educator input) and eventually adopt. Either the state or the Department of Education (DOE) in each district then crafted the curriculum "framework" to be followed in order to meet those standards.

Obama's blueprint seeks to bring US academic standards in line with international standards and suggests that states may do one of three things:

- They may revise their current standards, working collaboratively with their own institutions of higher education.
- They may join forces with other states to develop common standards.
- Or, they may choose the third option, which is to adopt the newly-created Common Core State Standards.

Most states have signed on for this third option. I'll explain:

In June of 2010, the National Governors Association Center for Best Practices and the Council of Chief State School Officers published a set of state-led education standards, the Common Core State Standards. They developed the Core Standards in collaboration with teachers, school administrators, and education experts and are based on an international standard. Don't worry - you won't be tested on this! Their names are not important. Their effect on your child's education is.

C.C.T. (Common Core Tweaked)

In 2015, Congress superseded the NCLB by passing the "Every Student Succeeds Act" (I know, it's like they're in a *Saturday Night Live* sketch!). This was an effort to undo the harmful effects of tying federal funding for schools to the implementation and testing of Common Core Standards.

Many states are still using the Common Core standards, but some that formerly adopted them have since rescinded their commitment, and a few have remained independent throughout the process. You can find out whether your state is currently using them by checking out the map on the Core Standards website: www.corestandards.org/in-the-states

SECTION TWO

YOUR CHILD'S BEST SELF

Let's sum up what we've covered thus far:

- You now understand the progression of your child's learning from grades K through 12.
- You understand standards and how your child is assessed with regard to these standards.
- You have seen examples of how this understanding can help a parent target her child's areas of strength and challenge.
- You understand what US educators' goals are for your child's development and how we got here.

Everything you've learned thus far provides the context you need to take action. Now that you know what happens in school (and why), you're ready to learn the in-school and at-home tools that will set your child up to succeed in school.

This new section lays out:

- How your particular child learns most easily and efficiently;
- How to make homework as painless as possible;
- Study skills for efficient and effective learning for school and for life;
- How to invest your child in his own learning process;
- Additional obstacles to learning.

Whether she's five or fifteen, whether she's currently excelling or struggling (or is somewhere in between), and whether she is a typical learner or might also need additional supports (which I will cover in Section Three of this book), these strategies will enable your child to be her best student-self.

CHAPTER FIVE

LEARNING IN STYLE

As I've been writing this book, I've been living day-to-day with an eight year-old-son who is facing what is the most infamous challenge of third grade (cue Beethoven's 5th)–the multiplication table. I also vividly remember the trials of mastering math facts myself.

> Day 1 in My Failure to Become a Math Major in College:
> Uncle Fred: (with enthusiasm) Hey, let's review your times tables!
> 3rd Grade Me: (pointing out the window and exclaiming) Look! I think the fish are biting!
> Day 2 in My Failure to Become a Math Major in College:
> My Dad: Aren't you supposed to be memorizing those times tables? Why don't I quiz you?
> 3rd Grade Me: I have a tummy ache.
> Day 3 in My Failure to Become a Math Major in College:
> My Dad: You know, you can't go through life without learning your times tables. Let's just give it a try.
> 3rd Grade Me: (as I run screaming from the room) NOOOOOOOOOOOOO!!!

Does this scene ring a bell? If you're like me, that challenge is one of the few that come back as clearly as if it happened yesterday. For that reason, it's a great lens through which to view the learning process. Most likely, your third grade teacher had his or her own particular way of teaching the times table, which may have made the whole experience a breeze for you, or on the other hand, may have made you feel the times tables were a mountain you would never summit.

In addition to drilling the facts at school, you were probably asked to work on them at home. What strategies did you use at home to burn those numbers indelibly into your head? I bet if you compared notes with a few of your friends and colleagues, you'd come up with a variety of different answers: your best friend had an actual table of numbers taped up by her bed, the last thing she'd see before falling asleep at night; your co-worker remembers asking a parent or sibling to drill her out loud at breakfast; your husband paced the room while going over them in his head; your child's teacher sang the Schoolhouse Rock songs to herself over and over on the way to school.

Why does this matter? Simply because it demonstrates that people are comfortable learning in a variety of different ways. These ways or preferences are called learning styles, and they are not only the way you are most comfortable learning, they also examples of the ways in which your brain is most efficient at learning.

> Your child's preferred learning style is simply the way
> his brain most efficiently assimilates information.

It's a Matter of Diversity

Diversity has become a big buzzword in our education system, and taking diversity into consideration is slowly but surely resulting in positive changes in our schools.

But there is one area of difference that has been largely ignored in the classroom, and that is the diversity of *our brains*. Don't laugh! You know intuitively that it's true. The kind of diversity we have been struggling as a society to achieve addresses the intermingling of ethnicities, cultures, and socioeconomics; it involves fostering communication between people who are different in ways that tend to be situational. This is not to say that achieving this kind of communication and diversity is not important, because of course it is extremely important. But I am saying—and you may want to sit down here—is that as challenging as nurturing cultural, ethnic, and socioeconomic diversity may be, it is not quite as challenging as addressing the diversity of our brains. I'm talking about a different kind of difference, one that is innate and essential to who we are. I'm talking about differences in the way we think and learn, i.e., our learning styles.

But why does that matter for my child's success in school?

Almost all of us use every type of learning style to some degree; our modern lives demand that of us. But many of us are not equally balanced in our preferences about learning; the majority of people learn most efficiently in one style or in a particular combination of styles. Pinpointing a child's preferred style or styles can in some cases dramatically improve both his enjoyment of school his success there.

Whether your child is struggling with academics or simply looking for a more optimal learning experience, it's a good idea to investigate her learning styles. Knowing your child's preferred learning style or styles will give you insight into many aspects of her education, such as why she may be excelling in certain classes or with certain teachers, but not with others, why she may or may not do well on tests, and how she best handles homework, all of which we will discuss below and in subsequent chapters.

I also suggest that you find out your own learning style preferences. I know, you're thinking "Wait, *my* learning styles? Aren't we focusing on my child's academics here?" Yes, we are, and it may sound funny to say that your learning styles are important, too, but ask yourself these questions:

- Have you ever tried and tried to teach your child something, and after a long series of failed attempts finally broken through without knowing why?

- Does your child accept help with homework from one parent, aunt, or sibling more readily than from others?
- Does your child argue with you about where, when and how to study?

If the answer to any of these questions is yes, it may be due to a difference in learning styles. Knowing your styles as well as your child's will help you communicate better about academics. So let's delve into the specific styles and how they define ways we learn.

The VAK Way

Educators have defined different learning styles in various ways, but there is one basic idea that most teachers will be familiar with. We call it VAK. Here's what VAK stands for:

- Visual   Learns best by seeing and reading
- Auditory   Learns best by listening or speaking
- Kinesthetic   Learns best by touching, moving, or doing

Simply looking at this list might be an immediate revelation to you. If your child relies heavily on just one of these modes, it may be evident to you as soon as you think about it. But don't worry if nothing jumps out at you right away. You can determine your child's preferred learning style or styles quite easily using a simple test. In fact, you can do it right now! If you do a simple online search for learning style assessment. You will be presented with multiple free options to have your child take the assessment online. One website I recommend: EducatorPlanner.org. for a simple diagnostic tool that will help you and your child develop efficient strategies for successful studying.

If you're still unsure, or wish to delve into this further, you will find a number of other learning styles quizzes available online for free. They each take a matter of minutes and give you an answer with a click of the mouse. If you want to get a very clear picture or your child, do one or two of these and compare notes. Most likely a pattern will emerge which will make sense, given what you already know about your child.

I'm guessing your next question is, "Ok, now what?" Well, now we put this information to use, both in school and at home. Compare what you have discovered about how your child learns best with what you know takes place in the classroom and at home during homework time. Does the environment and method of teaching match your child's style? If not, what can you, your child, or your child's teacher adjust to make learning as accessible as possible for her? Now it's time to sit down, brainstorm with your child, and, if you opt to do an Individualized Learning Plan (ILP; see Chapter 8), also add some strategies to your child's ILP.

I am including in this chapter some great ideas to employ for each learning style, but remember – this is just a jumping-off point. You can pick and choose the strategies you find here that work best for your student, or, even better, invent your own!

Strategies for the visual learner:

- **Use visual aids!** For a child of any age, an actual visual representation is the best aid to learning for a visual learner. These can take many forms:
  - For all ages:
    - Illustrations!
    - Color-coding to highlight important information

    - Traditional charts and graphs (pie charts, bar graphs, tables, line graphs etc.)
    - Flash cards
    - Linking the visual image to the idea, such as a list of colors, in which each word is shown in its own color (e.g., the word "Blue" is in blue ink; "Orange" is colored orange, etc.)
    - Graphic organizers (there are many free resources for these online; here's one to start you off: http://www.eduplace.com/graphicorganizer/
  - For young children or for older children with attentional challenges,
    - Picture schedules are very effective ways of keeping them focused and on task.

  - For older students:
    - Flow charts (if yes, then/if no, then)
    - Mind maps – Also known as a word web, a mind map is a popular contemporary method organizing information. It's sometimes also called a spider map. There is usually a single word or concept at the center, and other words or concepts branching off of it. Here are a couple of examples of mind maps:

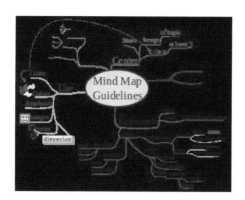

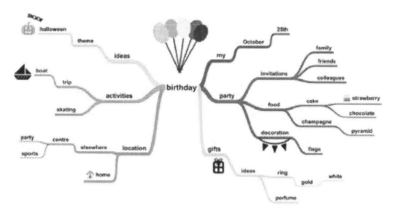

- Concept Maps – A concept map is a little more complex, and therefore better for older students. In a concept map, words and ideas are enclosed in circles or boxes and are linked to one another by connecting lines or arrows, according to their relationship with one another. The nature of the relationship between the words or concepts is written in linking words or phrases on the connecting lines. A concept map is harder to draw than a mind map, but can show much more complex ideas and relationships. Here's an example of a concept map:

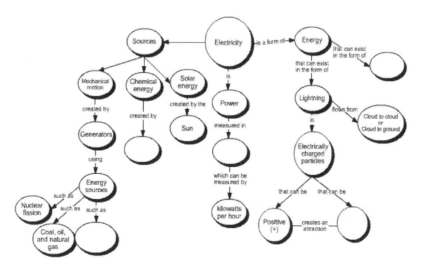

Find the type of visual aid that best suits the material and appeals most to your child. Having the child create his own visual materials is very beneficial. As your daughter copies out her flash cards, she sees it being written, which reinforces her mental picture of each spelling word she's trying to master.

- **Check out your study area.** Is it conducive to your child's dominant learning style? Visual learners are easily distracted by clutter or surroundings of visual interest. Your child probably will probably learn best in a calm, neat room with no TV. Make sure siblings' activities take place in a separate area. I will discuss this further in Chapter Five: Homework Happiness.

- **Provide your child with some eye-catching study goodies.** Highlighting a key idea in neon green or marking it with a striped mini-post-it will help her recall the visual image of the material that she will need to access later on.

- **Have your child copy out new math facts or vocabulary words onto index cards.** Consider using colored cards or writing with glitter pens on white cards. Glancing through the cards on the school bus or during lunch will reinforce the images – and hence the information – in her mind.

- **Use study intervals.** Encourage your child to study in 20- to 30-minute intervals and take short breaks in between.

- **Visualize the narrative.** For creative writing assignments, encourage your child to create a storyboard, laying out the story in pictures as a way to organize the plot.

- **Sharpen note-taking skills.** For older children, who in most schools are taught primarily thorough oral lessons or lectures, capturing classroom content can be tricky. Good note-taking skills will be your child's best asset. Make sure to take a look at Chapter Six, on Study Skills, for help with developing those skills. Interestingly enough, as the visual learner develops her note-taking abilities, she learns to listen for key points and connections and as a result also improves her auditory skills.

- **Enlist the teacher's help.** If your child's teacher does not expect students to take notes, but instead hands out prepared notes or outlines, encourage your child to explain to the instructor that he is a visual learner, and that it will help him absorb the lesson if he is given the outline or notes at the beginning of class so he can follow along or even highlight while listening. If the teacher does not commonly use outlines or visual aids (such as overhead projections or smart board images), it's ok – more than ok, it's responsible and great! – for the student to explain that he is a visual learner and to ask if the teacher could perhaps jot key concepts on a black- or whiteboard during the lesson. Most teachers will be impressed by a student's eagerness to learn and will be glad to make an effort to help him.

Strategies for the auditory learner:

For auditory learners, lectures are great! Your auditory learner can probably repeat everything his teacher went over in class each day. But much of the detail and supplementary information that supports spoken lectures or lessons is gleaned by reading and/or looking at visual information on a page. That's where your auditory learner will need the most support. This becomes more significant as your child gets older. That's because lessons for young children almost invariably contain visual or hands-on aspects, whereas the older your child gets, the more frequently he or she will be predominantly listening to a lesson.

Here are some strategies that can help your child at any age:

- **Create a study group!** If there is a particular subject that is heavy on reading, why not find others who are in the same boat and help each other out? A group of two or more kids can read chapters aloud to one another and discuss their ideas. This works at any age – You might be surprised to find that even young elementary school students can participate meaningfully in a study group.
- **Use a voice recorder.** See if your child's teacher is amenable to having him record lessons. That way, he can review the ideas at home later in a way that is much more accessible to him than reviewing notes.
- **Use the recorder at home, too.** Have your child read the assigned chapter into a recording device and then play it back for himself.
- **Read out loud.** If there are no classmates and no recording devices around, simply reading out loud instead of silently will help your auditory learner comprehend better and retain more information. In a public space like a library, reading 'out loud silently' by moving the lips and speaking just below a whisper will do the trick. At home, if the topic interests you, you could offer to read out loud to your child from time to time as well; that will allow you to start a discussion of the material, in which you can help your child think critically.
- **Take advantage of the web.** Find a podcast, audio TED talk, or Khan Academy webcast or other audio resource that covers the material. If you choose to use material outside of what is assigned, make sure your child okays it with his teacher, since the ideas or method of teaching may vary from what your child's teacher has planned. The instructor may even have a particular resource to recommend.
- **Ask for a lesson.** Have your child lecture you about the topic he's studying. Speaking the words aloud will be a good mnemonic tool to help him retain the material, and at the same time, he'll find out which areas he can explain to you easily and which concepts he needs to do a little more work on.
- **Sing!** If your child is having trouble memorizing something, suggest that she try putting the words to the tune of a song she likes, or that she compose a rap she can sing in her head to help recall the information.
- **Check out your study area.** Auditory learners have a wide range of optimal study circumstances. Some will benefit from listening to music while studying, while others will find it a distraction. In general, the more vocally interactive the study session can be, the better. This may mean the best study location for your daughter is at the kitchen island, reading highlights of her lesson to you while you chop up veggies for dinner.

Strategies for the kinesthetic learner:

I will not tiptoe around this fact: the kinesthetic learner faces the greatest challenges in today's formal educational system. I began this chapter comparing differences in the way kids learn to differences in race, ethnicity, culture, and socio-economics; that analogy fits the plight of the kinesthetic learner to a T. There are no two ways about it: every aspect of today's classroom discriminates against the kinesthetic learner. There is very little movement and hands-on in the classroom, and this is truer the older your child gets. The good news is that Common Core does address this inequity. That being said, it will take a very long time for teachers to adapt and change what they have been doing for the last 20-plus years. And in the meantime, you can do a lot to help your child not only get through school but also enjoy it – and you can believe me, because my own happy little whirling dervish of a kinesthetic learner loves to go to school!

- **Talk to your child's teacher!** Of course, as I say over and over, in almost every chapter of this book, communicating with your child's teacher is paramount to getting the best outcome in the classroom. This is especially true here – While auditory and visual learners will most often find that there is some aspect of the lesson that supports their learning styles, the kinesthetic learner (except during P.E. and dance classes) is often left with nothing to grasp–pun intended! Just bringing your child's learning style to the teacher's attention should help. An experienced teacher will have many resources on which to draw in order to work effectively with your child. If this turns out not to be the case, you can suggest ways that the teacher can support your child's learning in class, using your own understanding of what helps her. If classroom jobs are assigned, perhaps hers could be related to lessons, rather than handing out cups at snack time.

- **Help your child design study methods that include movement and touch.** Here are a few examples:
  o Allow him to use a calculator, an abacus, or manipulatives for math; ask his teacher to allow him to use small manipulatives or a mini abacus at his desk during math time in school (with Common Core in place, manipulatives are now a standard part of classroom instruction; they are also included as instructional tools on new Common Core online-based assessments used by most states (Smarter Balance or PARCC);
  o Adapt the mind map or concept map – See the descriptions of mind maps and concept maps above, in the visual learner section; You can adapt this study tool for your kinesthetic learner by having him write up each idea on a card. He can move the cards around on a large board until they are arranged in a way that makes sense, then glue them in place. At the office supply store, you can find small colored card stock shapes that are perfect for this activity.
  o Adapt the storyboard activity, also described above. Provide 'frames' in which your child can draw parts of his story (unlined index cards are perfect for this). Again, he will be able to move the cards around, adding, adapting and removing plot points, until he is ready to glue them down in the order he likes best.
  o Learn vocabulary or spelling words while jumping on the bed or a small trampoline.

- **Encourage lab work!** Your child's best learning opportunities in school will often be in labs, where everything is hands-on. If your school is not providing many lab opportunities, perhaps you can supplement some at home. If you find out what your child is learning about in science (and often math), a quick web search will often lead you to a hands-on activity you can do at home to support what he's learning in class. Here are a couple helpful links:
  o http://scifun.chem.wisc.edu/homeexpts/homeexpts.html
  o http://pbskids.org/zoom/activities/sci/

- Be flexible about the study location. You daughter really might get the most out of her reading assignment if she does it while swaying lightly in a backyard swing; your son might have the easiest time with his math if he and his paper and some manipulatives are sprawled on the floor.

While reviewing these suggestions, you will probably think up your own ideas. That's great! A custom-made strategy is often the best kind. For example, Tommy, a smart young man I worked with, was struggling with memorization. Tommy brought home top grades in many complex areas of study, such as Social Studies and English Literature, and was the 6th grade phenom of his Jr. high varsity basketball team. But Tommy had the hardest time memorizing tough spelling words and had never completely mastered his math facts, which brought his grades down in math, despite the fact that he understood the concepts quite well. When Tommy and his parents sat down with me to strategize, we all took a look at his learning styles quiz. Tommy had two strong learning styles: visual and kinesthetic. We realized that until now, he had been relying on his visual learning style for memorization. But for some reason, it just wasn't clicking. It was Tommy himself who came up with the idea of hooking into kinesthetic learning for memorization. He started going over his math facts and spelling words while practicing his basketball moves under the hoop in his front driveway. Tommy's Dad helped out by putting up big poster board signs on the garage door with times tables and spelling words, written in big letters, bringing his other learning style into play. Within a few weeks, Tommy's grades in math matched the rest of his subjects, and he stopped losing points on written reports due to misspelled grade-level words.

A Seat at the Table for Every Type of Learner (at the Times Table, that is)

For the Visual Learner: Help your child make herself some super-fancy flash cards – the flashier the better! Now is the time to break out those glittery gel-pens. Don't just use numbers on your cards—use colors and pictures, too.

For the Auditory Learner: Find the right CD! Your auditory learner will be chugging along on math facts with the right multiplication songs. There are many out there. One popular choice that I like is Multiplication Unplugged by Sarah Jordan Publishing.

For the Kinesthetic Learner: Play Power Towers! You can find many versions of this on the web, but simply explained, you take a sleeve of small bathroom cups and write the math facts on them. The problem (8x9= let's say) is written on the bottom of the cup and the answer (ummm, 72!) is written inside. The child takes a cup off the top of the stack, and if she gets the answer "in a snap", she gets to stack that cup in her tower; if she's a bit slow or gets it wrong, it goes back to the bottom of the pile. Depending on how many cups you've put in the pile, your builder can end up with quite a pyramid! One thing I love about this game is it can be played alone or in pairs.

For the Visual/Auditory Learner: Find the right music video! YouTube is crowded with music videos for just this purpose. My favorite is still the good ol' Schoolhouse Rock series.

For the Visual/Kinesthetic Learner: Find the right video game! I'm not kidding – The visual interest and the need to type keys to give your answers are the perfect combo for your learner. You can find numerous free games online with a simple web search using 'free multiplication games' (for instance, I like Underwater Math and Baseball Math at What2Learn.com, and Space Race at Multiplication.com).

For the Auditory/Kinesthetic Learner: Get your basketball and get outside! Recite the tables out loud as you dribble the ball, making use of the rhythm to put the sound of those number in your bones. If you're a good player, you will be able to challenge yourself by speeding up your dribble and trying to keep the math facts going with each bounce.

You are probably wondering by now why I haven't mentioned reading and writing in any of the above sections – after all, reading and writing are undoubtedly the most common modes of learning in schools and in society. Well, reading and writing hold a very special place in our learning process. First of all, because the read/write mode is in play all around us every hour of the day, and because we cannot function in our lives without it, we get quite a lot of constant practice at adapting to this mode, even if it doesn't suit us perfectly. I addition, the read/write mode relates to all three of the VAK learning styles: reading silently is a visual activity; reading aloud or listening to someone else read is an auditory activity; and writing is a visual and kinesthetic activity. Because of this, VAK is sometimes adapted as VARK, with Reading/Writing as a fourth learning style.

So wait a minute, these VAK/VARK styles you just told us about are not definitive?!

Nope. In fact, if you do a quick online search, you'll discover there are many different systems of defining learning styles. I started off introducing you to VAK because it is the most commonly used and referred to, and the most likely system your child's teacher will know of and how to address.

That being said, you may find some valuable insights about yourself and your child by checking out some of the other systems. My favorite system – and one I think can be very useful for parents and students trying to adapt homework and study skills – breaks down learning styles into seven preferences. Four of these correspond to VAK/VARK, which we have already discussed:

- **Visual/Spatial** — Corresponds to the visual learner
- **Aural/Auditory-Musical** — Corresponds to the auditory learner
- **Physical/Kinesthetic** — Corresponds to the kinesthetic learner
- **Verbal/Linguistic)** — This is the Reading-Writing Learner, who learns best doing verbal and linguistic activities.

But here are the three additional styles, which as you can see, add another layer of insight:

- **Solitary (Intrapersonal)** — This student learns best when working alone.
- **Social (Interpersonal)** — This student learns best when interacting with others.
- **Logical (Mathematical)** — This student loves logic, reasoning, systems, and math.

You can see a more detailed representation of all seven of these learning styles and some of the strategies that compliment them in the infographic below:

LEARNING STYLES: SEVEN WAYS TO LEARN

Visual/Spatial

- All about information presented visually
- Graphs, charts, maps, and color-coding can help organize information in a person's mind

Auditory

- Learning through sounds
- Music, rhythms, and speech patterns help learners remember important information

Verbal/Linguistic

- Information transmitted through words (written or spoken)
- Reading and listening are common ways to learn, and many people find speaking to themselves a good way to organize information

Kinesthetic

- Using one's body to learn
- Working with your hands, especially taking things apart and putting them back together, can be a powerful way to learn

Logical/Mathematical

- Numbers and patterns are key for learning mathematically
- Systematic and organized thinking helps people sort through lots of information

Interpersonal

- Learning with others
- Working through problems with the input of others can help people gain insight and feedback

Intrapersonal

- Working on your own
- Thinking through problems alone can help people organize their thoughts and sort through their ideas

Obviously, there will be many, many times, especially in the classroom, when your child's preferred learning style cannot be accommodated. This is plainly evident when we compare the solitary and social learners; The solitary learners will have to develop strategies to keep himself engaged in group work that is regularly assigned in class, while the social learner will her have to become comfortable with sitting quietly doing independent reading and written response, another common classroom experience.

Nevertheless, the student who knows herself and her preferred learning styles can often adjust many aspects of study to her needs. This is especially true at home.

Let's look at three examples of kids acknowledging their learning styles in order to meet academic challenges:

- Jamey is a kinesthetic social learner. She kept her eyes open and watched her classmates in American History, picking out three she thought had similar styles. The week before the AmHist midterm, Jamey invited these three kids over to her house after school for a game of American History Jenga.

- Gil is a solitary visual and read/write learner. He was placed in a group of 4 kids during Chemistry lab. Gil offered to be the recording member of the group, knowing that writing down the experiment's steps and results would help him retain the information. When he got home that night, Gil created a full-color chart detailing the experiment and its results as a way to review. He was his group's hero when he printed brought to school copies to share with everyone.

- Marcella is a logical, auditory learner whose spelling was atrocious. After we pinpointed her learning style profile, she and I came up with a plan to make her a spelling champ. We found a text that focused on word families and bought an inexpensive voice recorder. Marcella wrote and sang into the recorder a rap for each word family that laid out its spelling rules and cited some examples of their spellings. Since they were word families, they often rhymed, which worked perfectly for her rap. Marcella has now begun to see a pattern in the design of the English language, and her spelling has improved. Her teacher even asked to borrow a couple of her raps!

Understanding your child's preferred learning styles is a helpful tool in supporting him to be his best academic self. This valuable piece of self-knowledge will be especially relevant as you approach the next chapter, Homework Happiness, since it is in the home where you and your child have the most freedom to exploit his most effective and efficient methods of learning.

CHAPTER SIX

HOMEWORK HAPPINESS

Homework. There - I've said it . . . and I felt you cringe. It's a dirty word in so many households, the cause of more fights between parents and children than there are parents and children *on the entire planet.*

OK, not quite, but nearly. Homework is one of the leading sources of friction between parents and children. But it need not be. Whatever your personal opinion about the importance of homework, homework is simply a fact of life - of your child's life, that is - and while you can't (and, believe me, shouldn't) do it for him, there are many things you *can* do to set your child up to have an easier time with homework, to spend less time soldiering through it, and to gain a host of important life-skills in the process .

So let's map out what YOU can do to end the fights and frustration and to help your child have a good homework experience today, tomorrow, throughout his academic career . . . and beyond.

Attitude

While I'm sure many of you "get attitude" from your kids about doing homework, that's not the "attitude" to which I'm referring in the header to this section. I'm talking about *your* attitude towards your child's homework. The first and most important thing you can do is to adopt a positive attitude towards it yourself, and the calmly firm position that it is important.

Within reason, of course, the more aligned you are with your child's teacher's and school's specific messaging about homework, the better. The message needs to be that homework is important, and you must not undermine that message by saying such things as "yeah, I can't believe your teacher's giving you so much" (though we'll discuss this further later, because sometimes the teacher *does* give too much! I'll help you know how to determine this.). Parents who wish to curry favor with their children, to appear "cool," or to bond with them often erroneously pick homework as the common enemy to unite against with their children, putting it down as "stupid" and "a waste of time." But sadly, being a buddy with your child about this doesn't help either of you. Homework cements and furthers what she is learning in school, and if she thinks that *you* think homework is bogus, she'll use your ambivalence as a reason not to do her work well or not to submit the work on time... and she will suffer for it in both the short term and the long run.

"Yes, but. . ." you interject here, quite reasonably, "what if the amount of homework being given *is* too much?" Good question!

How to Know Whether the Amount of Homework Given is Appropriate

No question about it, the amount of homework students receive has increased since you and I were in school. Studies have been done on the efficacy of homework, and experts have established "The Ten-Minute Rule," i.e., that homework should ideally increase by ten minutes per grade. So - a first grader would spend approximately ten minutes per day on homework, a second-grader, twenty minutes, a third grader, thirty, etc. This is, however, only a guideline, and, in fact, many students in upper grades face far more nightly homework than the guideline recommends.

Most schools have homework policies. It's useful to ask your child's teacher just what that policy is. And then you want to follow up by asking your child's teacher how much time she expects your child to be spending on homework.

> Experts agree that time spent on homework should start with
> ten minutes in first grade and increase by ten minutes per grade.

Her answer to this question is useful information for you:

If your child is spending far *less* time than the teacher thinks the work should take but is getting the work done properly, your child is not challenged enough by the work.

- If your child is spending *less* time and is *not* getting the work done properly, he is zipping through the assignments without paying enough attention.
- If your child is spending far *more* time than the teacher estimates, it might suggest one of several possibilities:
    o Perhaps the homework zone in which your child is working has not been optimized (I will explain this below);
    o Perhaps your child is not focusing well (is music or the television playing while your child is doing homework? Are there other distractions? Again, I will explain this further, below);
    o Perhaps the homework itself is pointing to areas of challenge for your child;
    o *Perhaps the teacher is underestimating the time it takes to do the homework.* This does sometimes happen, and it's a simple matter to determine: Contact parents of your child's classmates to ask how much time their children are spending on homework from this teacher. Are other children spending as much time as your child, or is your child the only one logging so much time each evening? You'll quickly get the big picture and will see where your child fits into it. You may all discover that the teacher is underestimating how much time her homework assignments take to complete.

To clarify what I wrote above, if – and only if – you already have established firmly with your child that homework is important and must always be a priority, and if you *then* suspect that your child is, in fact, receiving too much, it is then OK to share with your child that you will be speaking with her teacher about the matter. It's fine under these circumstances to let your child know that

- you recognize her efforts;
- you see that she herself cares about her homework product but is spending what seems like an unduly long time on her assignments; and,
- you will be touching base with her teacher to discuss the matter.

This is wholly different than "jumping in the hole" with your child. This is not poo-pooing homework or griping about it along with your child in a way that will undermine her success, as I described above. Rather, this is about throwing her a rope and helping her learn to climb up and out. And up some more…

The message needs to be clear and consistent: Homework must be done

- well;
- without distraction;
- in a timely fashion;
- without fail.

Your child will get it. If you're firm about the parameters, your child will work within them . . . especially once you show them you mean business, by setting your child up to succeed.

Once you're clear about your message regarding homework, it's time to put that message into action by Scheduling Homework.

Scheduling Homework?

Yes, scheduling homework. Think about it: You schedule everything else in your child's week, right? Piano lessons are on Thursdays at 3:30, basketball practice and games are on Mondays-Thursdays right after school, swim lessons are on Saturday mornings . . . you get my drift. These are important, but, as we've established, so is homework, and if it is not scheduled as well, it will wind up being done as an afterthought, in a catch-as-catch-can way, if at all. It will wind up being rushed because it is being wedged into whatever time is left over after all the activities for which time has already been carved out. The work product will reflect that the homework was not a priority.

So - one of the first things you can do for your child is to make a calendar and post ALL of the scheduled activities. . . including homework time. If your child is young, you should schedule the time for him; if your child is older, you can guide him in doing so for himself. I like the large dry-erase calendars that you can put up in a visible spot. You/your child can write the Homework Times on it, and you/your child can also write in the actual assignments and cross them off as they're completed. At the end of the week, you can wipe them all clean with a rag and start afresh.

Obviously, things will come up, and you will need to be flexible. But that doesn't mean setting aside the schedule; on the contrary, it means *revising* it, so that the schedule reflects that you've still set aside time for the completion of your child's homework (another reason the dry-erase calendar is so handy-dandy - it's easy to revise!). As with scheduling homework to begin with, when your child is young, you yourself will mark down the birthday party or ballet recital that has arisen during homework time and will also mark down the new time during which homework will be done. And when your child is older, when a scheduling conflict arises you will guide him in firmly rescheduling his homework for another reasonable time himself. This not only helps create good homework habits, but it's also a way to foster independence by giving him some control: "You can go to that party, but then when will you do your homework? You need to schedule that in writing on the calendar before you can go."

Another aspect to flexibility is the importance of determining when is truly the best time for your child to do homework. It should be at an hour when the child is able to focus and do good work. For example, my friend's third-grader is at his freshest and most focused first thing in the morning but loses focus dramatically as the day goes by. And so, since he is a very early riser, she actually permits him to do his homework in the morning before school (and other parents I know permit their children to split their homework and complete some at night and some the next morning) My friend knows that her child is up early enough to complete it, he never fusses about doing his homework the way he would the evening before when he's tired and crabby, and it takes him only a third of the time it would take him to complete his work were he to do it in the afternoon or evening. Mind you, while this timing works for him, it wouldn't work for most kids. And she acknowledges that this may not work for the long-term projects her son will be assigned when he is older. But kudos to my friend for her willingness to be open-minded about what might, in fact, be the best homework schedule for her particular child at this time.

One more aspect of calendaring homework that is important for middle-school and high- school students is that of creating milestones for long-term projects. It is very helpful to get your child into the habit of breaking down an assignment into its component parts and scheduling each part. A book report due in two weeks? Schedule when the book will be read, when an outline will be written, and when the report itself will be written, using the outline as a guide. Have your child write everything down on the calendar, so that she sees exactly what she must do to get that book report done by its due date. She will feel "on top of" the assignment, and it will feel very rewarding to her to hand it in without having been through the last-minute panic so many children go through who have not broken down their long-term homework assignments into component parts and scheduled them.

I recommended *two* dry erase calendars for Casey, a very busy high school client of mine who competes nationally in gymnastics competitions and who came to me when her grades began to suffer. Casey now has a dry-erase weekly calendar on which all her activities and homework are scheduled; she also has a year-long dry-erase calendar on which she logs important competitions (and the extra practice and travel that they entail) as well as long-term projects for school, which are in planned out in minute detail. Casey is now often ahead of her classmates in each stage of a long-term project, because she knows she needs to stay on top of them if she wants to succeed both at school and at the gym.

Now that you've created the "when" of Homework, it's time to create the "where". . .what I like to think of as "The Homework Zone."

The Homework Zone

Most educators who specialize in study skills ask that every child have a dedicated Homework Zone where she does her homework every day. The key is to create an optimal setting that will minimize distraction, aid in focus, and facilitate the homework- doing process. If the environment is too chaotic, the child can't learn. Every time the child has to get up to go find a supply she needs, her focus has been disrupted and it will take time for her to re-establish her attention to the task she's been assigned.

Let's break this down for you:

The Setting

You might think that your child should be working at a desk in his or her own room. Not necessarily!

First of all, not everyone has space to spare in their homes for a desk, nor can everyone afford to buy desks for their children, and it's truly OK not to buy one if you can't - desks are not prerequisites for success at doing homework. And secondly, a child's room, full of fun distractions and away from the watchful eye of a parent, is not always the best place for him to work. Not yet, and, perhaps, depending on the child, not ever. Doing homework in his own room is a privilege your child should earn over time, once he has established great homework habits.

KIDS NEED TO EARN INCREASES IN AUTONOMY!

As with any increase in autonomy, your child needs to earn it by showing that he is ready for it.

How does he do this? By showing over time that he has established good homework habits, by doing his homework without grumbling and without being easily distracted, and by doing the assignments completely and well. As a rule of thumb, I do not recommend that children below the fourth grade be allowed to do their homework in their rooms in isolation.

If your older child begins campaigning to do his homework in his room and you think he might be ready, you can give him a one- or two-week trial period to see how it goes. Check in on him frequently to be sure he isn't just watching reruns of his favorite shows, surfing YouTube videos or playing video games on his computer. He'll either rise to the responsibility or he won't; letting him know in advance that you will be reassessing the situation on a week-to-week basis gives him the opportunity to earn this independence.

Small children, and even many older children, do best when doing their homework near a parent. The parent may be preparing dinner or may be doing homework of her own for work or further education. So when I say that a child must have a designated space in which to do homework, I don't necessarily mean a desk - that space may well be the kitchen table or kitchen counter. It should be well lit. If you are able to let your child have a say in selecting the designated spot, that's great, because it will give him a greater feeling of pride and investment in the space, which will increase his desire to be there.

The space should also be quiet, with a minimum of distractions. Any room in which a television, radio or stereo is blaring is not an option. There is an exception for this rule for particular children. As I described in the previous chapter, each child has his or her own learning styles profile. If your child is an auditory learner, you may discover that he actually has better focus with soft music or white noise in the background - just make sure there are no lyrics.

Whatever spot is selected should become The Daily Spot for doing homework - when homework begins, the dining room table, or small table in the family room, or kitchen counter becomes . . . The Homework Zone.

The Props and Supplies

So you've agreed upon the well-lit, quiet location that will become The Homework Zone during the times you've scheduled for each day, and you've minimized distractions during those times. Excellent! Now, to finish setting the scene, you need certain props and supplies. Many experts suggest that your child create a "Homework Zone" sign to put up during homework time, to transform what is normally a dining room table or kitchen counter into The Homework Zone. It's always best if the child makes and decorates the sign herself - it's a way for her to take ownership of the space and feel more invested in the homework process. Kids I know have had a lot of fun writing additional messages such as "KEEP OUT!" One talented child drew a truly menacing shark - I wouldn't have come within twenty feet, and I certainly wouldn't have attracted attention to myself by being noisy and distracting!

It is also very important to furnish the supplies your child needs. If your child is anything like mine, getting up every five minutes to "find something" he needs (a perfect excuse to delay), this will nip that in the bud. Every time a kid has to get up to go find something - colored pencils for a project, a ruler for math homework, an eraser - her focus has been shattered, and it will take a while for her to get back in action . . . and homework will take exponentially longer than it need take. If your child is sitting at a desk, it is easy to keep the supplies in the desk. If she is sitting at another space that gets transformed into her daily Homework Zone, however, it is every bit as easy to have her supplies in one place and on the ready. You can buy a bucket, bin, fishing tackle box . . .there are any number of things with handles and compartments that will do the job.

As for which supplies your child needs, it depends on her age. In their wonderful book, *Homework without Tears,* my favorite homework experts, Lee Canter and Lee Hausner, have created lists for different age groups. And if this chapter of my book whets your appetite for more information and tips on diminishing homework stress, I highly recommend reading their book in its entirety. For example, you may want to gather the following items.

What your child needs for a well-stocked study space:

Pencils

Pens

Erasers (The large, pink kind are the sturdiest.)

Pencil sharper (If you get hand-held, go with one that has a top to collect shavings)

Glue sticks

Ruler

Calculator

Ruled writing paper (Keep the same kind that is preferred by the teacher.)

Spiraled notebook

Dictionary

Scissors (appropriate for the child's age)

Other helpful supplies

These items, while not always necessary, are helpful to have on hand:

Colored markers

Paper clips

Tape

Four-ounce bottle of white glue

Index cards

Folders

Construction paper

Access to a printer

Homework Habits

We've discussed the "when" and the "where" of homework; now we really must discuss the "how."

If you've already scheduled the homework (the "when") and carved out your child's Homework Zone (the "where"), you've already taken meaningful steps to establish that homework is a priority. This will help your child do a better job of it. But there is more you can do to create good homework habits ("the how"), no matter how old your child. Let me restate this last part: Your child is never too old - it is never too late - to establish good homework habits.

As with doing the homework in a particular place and at a particular time, what you are trying to do is create good new habits that will become intrinsic with repetition over time. As with anything, this involves training, with rewards and supports that can be diminished until they are ultimately withdrawn altogether once the new behaviors have firmly taken root.

How do you do this?

- By firmly establishing the expectations in advance that homework will be done
- at a certain time,

- o in a certain place,
- o in a timely fashion,
- o independently,
- o thoroughly, putting forth a focused and good effort, and
- o without grumbling or negotiating.
- By creating a reward system for compliance with all of the above, that will gradually be faded out as the behaviors become second nature.
- By remaining calmly firm and consistent in your expectations.
- By holding your child to these expectations, with consequences for their failure to comply.

Don't worry - I will explain all of these steps!

Positive Feedback/Rewards

Let's discuss rewards. As with any training program in which you are trying to encourage new behaviors until they've become second nature, rewards are your friends.

All children feel good when praised, so praise is a great first-step reward. Has your child been sticking to the schedule? Praise him! Has your child been doing his homework in the Homework Zone? Great job! Has your child been getting his homework done in a reasonable amount of time? Excellent! Without pestering you for help every two minutes? Thumbs up! Has he been getting good feedback from the teacher for his efforts? Bravo!

But at least initially, when the behavior you are seeking is not the behavior your child wishes to perform, you will need more than praise alone. Setting up a system with your child, so that your child knows he is working towards a goal, will do wonders.

With younger children, a spinner is fun to use (see example below). You know, like the ones used in board games to determine how many spaces each pawn will move in its turn. I suggest to parents that they make spinners with numbers on them. (There's an app for that!) When the child accomplishes a particular goal (i.e., the child does her homework at the scheduled hour, or the child finishes her work in a timely manner), she gets to spin for points. When the child accumulates a certain number of points, she gets a coveted prize - perhaps she gets to stay up an extra 30 minutes on the weekend, or watch a movie she's been wanting to see, or download an app on your iPad that she's been keen to play. As long as it's meaningful to her, it will do the trick.

With an older child, you could use a spinner (and for certain pitfalls, described below, you may want to), or you could just keep track of what he's doing each night, marking them down on the schedule and checking them off or starring them when goals are met. If he accomplishes the goals you and he set out for a certain time period, he gets whatever reward has been predetermined by you both.

Don't undermine your aims by waiting so long to reward your child that the child loses steam. Younger children need more frequent gratification than older children do. A young child cannot wait a whole week for a reward, whereas an older child may be able to wait for two weeks. My rule of thumb is that little kids should see a reward every two or three days at most. Fourth and fifth graders can go for a week, while sixth-eighth graders can be expected to wait two weeks and high school students can take a month to earn a reward. If you expect a child to wait too long, the goal will feel unattainable, he will give up, and the behavior you are seeking to habituate will not become habit. Over time, though, as the new ways of doing homework do, in fact, become habit, you can offer fewer and fewer tangible rewards and the behaviors will still stick. Good homework habits will be in place that will put your child in good stead in all that he does in his life. Remember, though, that you need not reduce the level of praise you offer: praise doesn't cost anything and you have an unlimited supply of it, so if your child continues to do his homework well, keep that praise flowing!

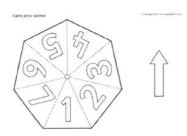

Timeliness

Some children take an unduly long time to complete their homework. If you have one such child, first, of course (as discussed above), you must determine whether the work is too difficult for your child (I will discuss in a subsequent chapter how to seek help for your child if he is struggling with grade-level work), or, possibly, whether the teacher is giving more than she thinks she is. If neither is the case, and your child just has difficulty focusing, I employ the chunking method: First of all, I create a spinner that has different rewards in each of the sections. These should be small-scale rewards, since the child may be spinning a few times over the course of the homework time. I divide the homework into chunks - five-minute sections, perhaps (or, for example, five questions/math problems per chunk), with mini-breaks in between. I fold over the page, so that the child only has to see one chunk at a time, which makes the task at hand feel far more manageable to him. If the child *does quality work* and completes the chunk in the time I've allotted for it, he gets to spin the spinner for a reward (You can also write out an index card with rewards and have the child toss a die.).

Children find this highly motivating. Furthermore, since the homework is divided into chunks, the child doesn't get overwhelmed by the amount he has to complete: "six five-minute chunks" seems far less daunting than "a thirty-minute assignment." The child develops greater confidence, as he sees that yes, he was able to complete the whole assignment. Over time, the child's focus will expand. He'll be able to go from five-minute chunks to ten-minute chunks without losing focus. . .and before you know it, the Problem of the Endless Homework Sessions will be a thing of the past.

Independence

Your goal is for your child to do her homework independently. So what do you do when you have a child who seeks your help every two minutes?

First, determine whether your child actually needs your help. If she does, that's OK! She may not have grasped the new concept that was taught in class that day. If this happens once in a while, simply help your child understand the concept, sit with her while she begins to use it, then leave her on her own again. On the other hand, the homework may simply be too difficult for her. If so, you will need to explore why this is so and what steps you need to take to help her catch up with her classmates. As I said, I will be discussing this at great length in the next section of this book.

If you are certain that your child understands the concepts and is fully capable of doing the homework on her own but simply wants to keep you hooked into her homework process, there is a technique I particularly like to use: At the beginning of Homework Time, place ten dimes (or quarters, M&Ms, chocolate kisses, skittles. . .whatever works) in a bowl. Tell your child that she may ask up to ten questions while doing her homework, but that for every question she asks, you will remove one dime (or whatever the item is -I'm calling it a dime). When she has finished her homework that evening, she may keep the dimes that remain. It becomes her choice: does she want the help that she doesn't actually need, or the money? Believe me when I tell you that the children catch on quickly . . . and before too long are planning what they want to do with their "hard-earned" dough.

Best Efforts

You also want your child to try hard and give his homework his best effort every time. But in their attempt to get homework over with as quickly as possible, many kids do a sloppy job. As with the children who are unfocused, I use chunking and a spinner, this time, the one with the different point values on it. If a child has twenty math problems to do, for example, I divide them into chunks of five problems, with mini-breaks in between, during which I look over the work. Unlike with the dawdler, above, the goal here is not speed, it is accuracy and thoughtfulness. If the work shows true effort, the child can spin for a reward. If not, the child must try that chunk again . . . at which point, if it's well done, he can spin for the reward.

Homework is Non-negotiable!

You must remain calm and clear about the message I stated at the top of this chapter. Your child may attempt to negotiate, may cry, may pitch a fit, or may even flat-out refuse to do her homework. It would be best for you to remain calm and not engage in any of it. Simply remain firm that the homework must be done before other, more desirable activities may be resumed. Period. And then stand by what you've said.

As I mentioned above, both rewards and consequences should be employed where necessary. Rewards are about building confidence. Consequences are about breaking bad habits and behaviors. You can give points towards a reward AND take points away . . .as long as you provide enough guidance and support to make the rewards attainable, so that your child will get that needed boost in confidence and will get into the habit of doing homework in the efficient and self-disciplined ways I've discussed above that will help her succeed.

By no means do I think that implementing the strategies in this chapter is easy. It can feel to many like having a whole second job. I understand. I will say, though, that while it may be hard in the short term, anything you do implement will help and, in the long run, will make life easier for your child . . .and yourself. Even if you just try one strategy at first that you feel is "do-able"... and then add another at a later time, when you and your child are ready . . .you will see improvement. Any step you take will be meaningful.

> It's ok to start small.
> Try implementing just one strategy that
> you feel is "do-able" for your family.
> Each successful strategy
> you teach your child
> will make his life – and
> *yours!* – a little bit easier!

Last Resort for Parents of Older Students: The Contract

For the parent at the end of your rope, who has tried everything with your older child: you can create a contract with them. The contract can contain a set of objectives, goals, and criteria that the child has to meet, with a tied-in, predetermined set of rewards and consequences. This is a serious document: the contract should be written out and signed by both parties.

Such a document can be a great tool. It gives the student a satisfying sense of control. The child knows the expectations, the goals, the rewards and the consequences in advance. The contract can be folded into a homework tracker - the teacher signs off on what the homework is each day, the student signs off later that she has done the work, and the parents sign off that they have reviewed it to see that it was done.

Is your child is acting cocky and overconfident? This is usually a charade to cover the fact that she's finding the material difficult. A child may not wish to do homework because she is afraid of being "found out" - she's afraid that her teachers and parents will discover her areas of weakness and she will be embarrassed or in trouble over it.

And so I encourage you to engage your child's teacher(s) in the contract, so that there is a whole team supporting your child in doing her homework more effectively. If you follow up the contract with the techniques I set out throughout this chapter -

- you buy that big dry-erase calendar on which you schedule daily homework time and you also schedule the various steps to completion of long-term assignments;
- you create a peaceful and well-stocked Homework Zone;
- you reward well-done completion;
- you stand firm with consequences for a failure to complete the work; and,

- your child's teacher is in on the whole process, helping to ensure that the child's assignments are written down and the necessary books come home at the end of the school day,

your child may find herself gaining true confidence and leaving the cockiness behind, as her ability to understand and execute her work improves.

New Habits for Parents, Too

It is important to understand that whether you use a contract (and whether that contract involves the homework tracker) or you are helping your child using the other techniques I've outlined above, *your follow-through in monitoring and staying abreast of your child's Homework Habits is every bit as important as what you're asking your child to do.* Otherwise, the whole process will become a pointless exercise.

I know what I'm proposing may seem hard to do, because I'm suggesting new habits for both parent and child. I will tell you, though, that it is most helpful to children when parents try to use the same strategies we're outlining in this chapter, so that their role in Homework Time becomes as much of a habit for themselves as the habits they're trying to develop in their children. I will also tell you that your one-time investment in developing these new habits will ultimately not only save you time but will also reduce conflict on an ongoing basis.

If you set up a homework schedule but fail to keep your child to it, *you've taught by example* that homework can be catch-as-catch-can. If you create a Homework Zone but your child persists in doing homework in front of the television while her brother's practicing the violin and you're talking on the telephone, you're sending a strong message that homework simply isn't important. If you insist that homework be given your child's best effort, but you don't check to see that it is, or you fail to follow through on promised rewards for timeliness, your child will not develop the habits you wish for him, and the struggles will simply continue. If, however, you do exhibit self-discipline in implementing these techniques, your follow-through will become habit for you, just as your child's better homework practices will become habit for him.

And life will get easier . . .it really will. I promise.

CHAPTER SEVEN

BEYOND HOMEWORK: GOOD STUDY AND TEST-TAKING SKILLS

Remember Naya, whom I discussed in Chapter 3? Of course you remember - super-social Naya, who was smart and well-liked, but was struggling by junior high and drowning by high school, because she lacked basic study skills . . . ?

Hopefully, the chapter on Homework that you just read can help you set up your child with habits that will serve her throughout her school career . . . and beyond, into the workplace. But most of what I discussed in the previous chapter had to do with forming good study habits and developing organizational skills. In this chapter, I will introduce you to the essential study skills that your child needs to succeed in her studies, both at home and at school. Naya would have benefitted greatly from mastering these skills long before she came to me in her junior year.

It's easy to overlook these, to assume that our children know how to be students, how to do the basic tasks that students are asked to do. But there is an art to doing these tasks - an art which, sadly, is rarely taught in schools -and it's not hard to help your child become a master artist.

I'm talking about how to:

- Listen in class;
- Take good notes in class;
- Read a textbook;
- Memorize;
- Prep for Tests; and
- Organize.

My friend George used to talk about approaching everything with what he called, "The Salami Technique." If someone handed you a whole salami to eat, you'd think, "I could never eat that entire thing!" But George would say, "Sure you can! Just use the salami technique!"

So what, exactly, is the salami technique?

With a grin, George would answer: "One slice at a time."

Let's take good study and test-taking skills One Slice at a Time, starting with the two in-class slices:

Listening in Class

You might want to check in with your child's teacher to find out how engaged your child seems to be during lessons. Is your child sitting up and facing forward, in a way that indicates that your child is actively listening? Does your child participate, asking or answering questions? Is your child animated during projects done with other children? Or does your child slouch, lean back, gaze away, seemingly disinterested in the topic being taught?

The very first study skill to look at is your child's listening - don't take it for granted that your child is paying attention. If you find that the child is unfocused in class, you will want to talk with the teacher about it. Perhaps the child should be seated in a different part of the room. Perhaps the teacher can make a point of asking the child specific questions that can help keep him on track, or, for a younger child, can give him a special "job" to do (write key points on the blackboard, for example), that will keep the child motivated and "in the game."

Further steps can be taken if it seems that your child actually has trouble focusing in class. A lack of focus is quite often not your child's choice. . .and there is much that can be done to help him. I will discuss this further in later chapters.

And even if your child is, in fact, paying attention, don't assume that your child knows what to listen for. Teachers talk a lot - how can your child know just which tidbits to pay the most attention to, among all those things that are being said?

Teachers give cues about what is most salient, i.e., most important to know. You can call these cues "clues," you can deputize your child to be a detective who will be searching for these "clues," and you can prep your child to listen and look for them. Here are some of the "clues" your child can be searching for, which indicate that something is important to know:

- Any time your child's teacher says, "Write this down," your child should not only write down what follows, but should also make a mental (and literal!) note that it is important to know the content!
- Teachers will often say outright, "This is important," in which case, it is! Such phrases as "Importantly," "Most important," and "The basic concept is . . ." are variations on that theme.
- Similarly, they'll often say, "Remember ..." Don't assume your child's ears perk up at that word. Tell your child that this is a clue to listen for.
- Teachers will give an introductory statement that helps students make sense of what will follow. An example: "There are two types of trees . . ." Your child should now listen for the first, followed by the second. And your child should be expecting to hear what defines each of these two types and what differentiates the one from the other.
- Similarly, any time a teacher says, "First ...," "Second ...," "Third...," etc., she is signaling that an important idea is to follow.
- "Because" and "So" are generally followed by ideas to remember.

- Teachers will often repeat something important, and will often lead in with "Let me repeat…," or "Again," a definite clue that your child should consider the repeated tidbit something worth knowing.
- Any time your child's teacher says, "To summarize," "In conclusion," "In summary," "Therefore," or something like that, your child's ears should perk up, and she should listen carefully to the summary that follows - that summary will contain the facts, themes and conclusions the teacher considers most important!
- Anything at all that the teacher ever goes to the trouble to write on the blackboard or put up on the smartboard is important information!

These might seem like obvious cues to you, but trust me when I tell you that they're not obvious to many children. So review them with your child. Kids like being detectives, so they 'll enjoy the challenge of listening for these cues. Furthermore, children who didn't already know to listen for these words will feel empowered by the tip - they'll feel more competent and more in control of how they' re learning, and this actually makes a world of difference in the attention they pay in class.

Text Detectives

I mentioned that kids like being detectives. In fact, according to David Coleman, an architect of Common Core, kids need to be "reading like detectives and writing like investigative reporters." The goal of teaching what is called "close reading" is to promote deeper reading and greater critical thinking based on evidence found in the text. Children are encouraged to look for clues, ask questions, make a case, and, finally, prove it with details from the text.

Saving the "Best" for Last

Another important pointer you can share with your child is that the very last few minutes of class can sometimes be the most important: a teacher will either try to rush through material he didn't manage to cover in class but had wanted to, or he may use those minutes to recap the most important points he did cover. Either way, even if your child may have done a great job of paying attention for most of the class, she needs to be careful not to "reward" herself by letting her attention wander in those last few minutes.

You can also ask your child's teacher outright what he does to let children know what will be covered on tests. Perhaps the teacher gives review sheets - you can then go over those review sheets with your child. Sometimes the mere fact that you've asked the teacher this question can help focus the teacher and will motivate him to give the children such a review sheet or summary, or even a practice test.

Note-Taking in Class

By middle school, students are usually expected to be taking notes in class. This is a skill that needs to be taught, but, once again, it usually isn't.

Good news! Teaching your child how to take effective notes will have the added benefit of helping your child listen well in class - isn't that great?!

And I must reiterate that giving your child a system for taking good notes will boost his confidence in the classroom in a very meaningful way.

But how should students take notes effectively and efficiently?

In preparation for taking notes:

First of all, I recommend that your child use loose-leaf binders and paper, rather than bound notebooks. This will enable your child to add or remove notes, and to punch holes into and add in hand-outs the teacher gives on particular days, related to particular topics.

Second of all, your child should start a new page each day and should put the date at the top of that page. She can then number the consecutive pages for that date, e.g., November 26 at the top of the first page that day, then 11/26, p. 2 at the top of the next, 11/26, p. 3 at the top of the next, etc.

And, lastly, if your child is completing homework properly, he will come to class having read the materials the teacher assigned for that day, which will help him follow the class discussion. More about textbook reading, below!

Now as for how to actually take notes:

First of all, your child should NOT think that she is supposed to write down every word the teacher says. Remember those "clues" that your child is going to be listening for? Reviewing those types of words and phrases with your child will help him understand that these are the markers to listen for, because they indicate that what the teacher is about to say is worth writing down. Your child should write down enough of the idea to remember what it is, instead of trying to write the whole sentence that the teacher said. For example:

TEACHER SAYS: There are two types of trees:

STUDENT WRITES: 2 kinds

The student is then ready to write the two types below:

TEACHER SAYS: The two types are coniferous and deciduous.

STUDENT WRITES: 2 kinds > conifrus / decidus

And so on.

Second, our child's notes are the one place where spelling doesn't count! In fact, your child should abbreviate where possible. Every child I know has come up with his own little abbreviations for commonly written words. "Bee" for "because," "w/" for "with," and these days "@" for at are common ones, but you'd be amazed what your child will invent for words he finds he has to write a lot. Whatever works for him is fine, as long as he himself remembers what his own abbreviations stand for!

Third, your child should write on only one side of each page (sorry, trees!), so that he can put the pages side by side when studying, to see through-lines and connections that might be helpful.

And,

Fourth, if the teacher is saying something your child doesn't understand:

1) YOUR CHILD SHOULD ASK THE TEACHER TO EXPLAIN IT! Children do not always realize that they are entitled to do so! If the child asks, but still doesn't understand what the teacher is saying,
2) Your child should put a question mark in the margin of his notes, to signal that this is something he's going to need further explanation about. He can then go to the teacher in private to get the needed clarification(s).

And, finally, after the notes have been taken in class:

I know this next tip is not an in-class tool, but it goes hand-in-hand with in-class note-taking, so I'll add it here. Not everyone will do this, but I cannot stress strongly enough what a powerful tool this is:

Your child 's understanding of what she is learning in school will be strengthened enormously if she rewrites her class notes each evening, just prior to doing her homework assignments. Doing so will provide a review that will solidify her grasp of the information, which will make it easier for her to do her homework. . .which she will then do more quickly as a result. It will also give her a chance to clarify, flesh out, correct and enhance what she wrote in haste in class . . .which will not only make it easier for her to understand the next material being taught, but will also make it easier for her to study when test-time comes around. Since she's using that handy loose-leaf binder I suggested, she will now be able to replace her messy notes with the clean, fleshed-out version right in the correct order with the rest. Another option that works for a lot of kids is to rewrite their notes onto note cards.

Lefties, Take Note!

It's often more of a challenge for left-handed students to take good notes than it is for their right-handed peers. Every notebook and binder is designed specifically for the use of the right-handed note-taker. This is a backwards world your lefty is used to by now, but that's no reason she needs to suffer. Remember that although assignments must be written starting on the front of a loose-leaf page (and that's ok, because your child can remove the paper form the binder and write on a flat surface) does not mean that notes must be taken the same way. Notes are for your child's use only. Your southpaw can simply write on the backs of the loose-leaf sheets rather than the fronts, or the backs of spiral notebook pages, so that the binder rings or spirals are not in her way. Or, as I wrote above, she can write on notecards that can then be hole-punched and put onto a ring or kept paper-clipped in a pouch.

That being said, the lefty note-taker still faces the inky mess that often results from the simple fact that she must still write from left to right (unless she's another Leonardo Da Vinci), dragging her hand across the freshly written lines as she goes. For this reason, a laptop or tablet is a welcome tool to the left-handed student. If your lefty is having trouble taking good notes, it could really just be the physical obstacles getting in her way - try the side-two-only method, or, if possible provide a digital solution.

And now that we've made our way outside the classroom, let's look at the skills you can help your child master at home:

<u>Reading a Textbook</u>

Let me say right off the bat that this section does not apply to math textbooks. They are their own breed of book.

All other textbooks tend to follow a particular pattern, and, while that pattern might be boring (OK, I've said it!), it does lend itself to a system that can make reading the content and retaining it - a snap for your child.

This method is widely touted, so trust me when I tell you that it works for all ages from middle school straight through college. (There are advanced steps for approaching the textbook as a whole when you first receive it, but I won't go into those here, since they're beyond what one would expect a middle- or high-schooler to do.)

For your middle-schooler or high-schooler assigned to read a particular chapter of a textbook:

1. She should first skim the entire chapter, paying particular attention to the section headings and any sentences written in bold, as well as to any photographs and their captions. This will give your child an overview of the entire chapter and, hopefully, a spike in interest in the material she's about to delve into.

2. STOP! If there are any vocabulary words listed, make sure that your child understands them before going any further!

3. She should then take the chapter one section at a time:

   a. For each section, she should first skim that section once more before reading that section more carefully. When skimming, she should again pay particular attention to the bolded words, phrases and sentences, as well as to the photos and their captions. (The heavily visual learner will benefit from the use of highlighter in this part of the process. The auditory learner may want to be reading into a voice recorder.)

   b. Once that section has been skimmed, she should STOP and take a minute to think about what that section was about.

   c. Then she should go back and read that section very carefully. (The auditory learner can play back his recording and listen while she reads along.)

   d. After her careful read, she should again STOP and take a moment to think again about the information she just read. If she can't remember what the section was about, she should reread it. It's OK - it happens to everyone!

   e. She may wish to write down the section header and any key words or ideas. This is optional, but I do believe it is very helpful to do.

4. She will then be ready to go on to the next section.

5. After skimming and reading each section, she should carefully read the chapter summary. Did it make sense?

6. If there are chapter questions at the end of the chapter (and there almost always are), she should write out her answers to them.

7. She should then go back into the chapter to find the answers to those questions and should check to see if what she's written is correct.

This may seem like a laborious process, but it's actually far more efficient than trying to read a whole chapter and then realizing you haven't retained a thing and going back and rereading the whole chapter but realizing that it was STILL too big a bite to chew and having to do it again . . .This system actually breaks down the chapter into bites that can be chewed, swallowed and digested. It's a good system, it really is. It really, really is.

Memorizing

Memorization of facts is just one of those aspects of school you can't get around. Students are expected to memorize facts, from multiplication tables to the dates of certain battles to the major export of Albania. Which is chrome (well, metals and textiles). Which I only know because of an episode of the classic sitcom "Cheers" in which young bartender Woody had to memorize the fact for a community college course he was taking, and he made up a song about Albania to help him remember the facts he was required to memorize.

The song worked. Scores of former "Cheers" fans remember that dopey little ditty. We not only know Albania's chief export, we know that Albania borders on the Adriatic and that its terrain is mostly mountainous, as well.

Why?

Here's what you need to know about memorization: Repetition and Fun are the keys to memorization.

Think about it: How many songs can you sing along to? How many song lyrics do you know? Hundreds? Actually, probably thousands, despite the fact that you never sat down to study and memorize any of them. So why do you know so many lyrics to so many songs?

1. the tune is catchy - it helps you remember the words; and
2. you liked the song so you listened to it over and over again.

So what does your child need to do to memorize? Your child needs to repeat information IN SMALL PIECES, over and over again. Your child needs to do this in as fun and engaging a way as possible.

If your child is very small, you can help her do so by saying the info and asking her to repeat it. You can get silly, saying it in silly voices and having her do the same. You'll both giggle a lot, but she'll remember what she's been asked to memorize. Just remember - what you're asking her to repeat must be SHORT. One small bit at a time. Only move on to another bit once your child has fully memorized the first bit. Trying to move her forward too quickly will slow her down in the long run, since she will get confused or frustrated . . . or both.

An older child can make flash cards, but make it fun for him to do so. He can illustrate the flash cards, he can make up games to play with the cards and teach you the game. He can make up songs, as Woody did about Albania. Or, with a series of items that need to be memorized in a particular order, he can make up a sentence with the first letter of each subsequent item in the sequence. A famous example is the planets:

Mercury, Venus, Earth, Mars, Jupiter, Saturn, Uranus, Neptune

My Very Educated Mother Just Served Us Noodles

(She used to serve us ". . .Nine Pizzas," but then Pluto was demoted to "dwarf planet").

Kids have fun making up their own silly sentences in such instances.

And, finally, another tried and true method is to put whatever needs memorizing on a large dry-erase board. Your child reads what's written several times. You then erase the first word . . .but your child still states aloud the whole sentence, supplying the erased word from memory. Your child does this several times . . . and then you erase the second word, and your child continues to state the whole sentence, supplying from memory the two words that are no longer there. This exercise is repeated until all the words have been erased, and the child can still state the whole string of words. It's an effective method. The trick, for me, is to still find a way to make it fun - this one is where incentives such as M&Ms or, perhaps, quarters, can keep your child engaged. Using funny voices or setting the whole statement to song as mentioned above makes this method more fun, too, and lends another layer of memorization-assistance to the process.

All of these methods engage your child's creativity and spirit of play while providing that critical component of repetition.

Take your child's learning style(s) into account when choosing memorization methods to try. The visual learner may do well making her own flash cards with many fancy colors and stickers; the auditory learner will enjoy word play, songs, and rhymes; the kinesthetic learner will benefit from rhythms and props. If you use the white board method, provide markers in a variety of colors and line thicknesses for your visual learner; make sure you and your auditory learner say the words out loud as you write them (and maybe even say them backwards as you erase them!); and allow your kinesthetic learner to do the writing and erasing himself, and to take a march around the white board between sections.

Prepping for Tests

I won't say much here about prepping for tests, because if you've already implemented the Homework Happiness techniques I laid out in the last chapter and have helped your child learn to employ both in class and at home the study skills I've just set forth in this chapter, your child actually should be well prepared for the exams his teachers give him. At this point, the very best things you can do to help your child are:

- Reassure him that he is, in fact, well prepared. Remind him of all he did to prepare, so that you're backing up your assertion with logic and facts. Kids respond well to this - they realize you're not just saying what they want to hear to make them feel OK because you're their parent.
- Make sure your child gets a good night's sleep, rather than staying up cramming for the exam. Again, if the homework and study skills techniques are in place, there is no need to cram.
- Make sure your child eats a good, nutritious dinner the night before AND DOES NOT SKIP BREAKFAST the morning of the test. And I need not tell you, my fellow parent, that a pop-tart does not a breakfast make.

As regards test-taking advice, you can advise your child on the following test-taking strategies:

- If the test is a timed multiple-choice test, AND if the test does not outright deduct points from the student's score for a wrong answer, AND if your child has managed to quickly narrow the choices down to two, she can guess, and move on. If not, she should leave it blank and hope to come back to it after completing the other questions. If, at the end of the exam, she is reviewing those problems and can answer the question, great! If (and only if!) she's still drawing a blank at the very end, then at that point she can simply guess and fill in any of the holes at random. And,

- Your child should never be handing in her test before the time is up -there is no such thing as "extra time" when taking a test. If your child has finished answering all of the test questions with extra time to spare, she should edit, "solve backwards" her math problems for accuracy, check grammar, and, of course, review her answers, - she may well catch a mistake or three.

Test-Taking Tips from the Trenches for Teens - SAT/ACT

A colleague of mine tutors students of all ages for summative tests that run the gamut from the third grade FCAS to the GED. I asked him for a few tips for high schoolers facing the dreaded SATs and ACTs. Here's what he said (speaking directly to teens):

Know Your Test! Each type of standardized test is scored a different way, and the scoring systems can change from year to year. Make sure you understand the scoring system so that you can make good choices about when to skip a question, when to make an educated guess at the answer (by eliminating one or two of the choices), and when to guess at random.

Know Your calculator! "Kids I tutor who know their calculators are at a huge advantage." In many cases, there is no limit on the type of calculator you are allowed to use. Find out the parameters and show up to the test with the best calculator you can afford or borrow. There is a big difference in the number of functions between a $5.00 calculator and one that costs $125 and up-It seems crazy that an expensive piece of electronics can affect your score, but it's true. The caveat is that the calculator can only help you if you know how to use it. Learn its more advanced functions and you will be way ahead of the game.

Tutors over classes, if possible. I know that if you are taking the SAT, you're about to go off to college - a daunting expense for your parents! - so forgive me for saying so, but if you are planning to get extra help for test prep, it is preferable if possible to choose a private tutor with excellent references over a class. There are many excellent classes, so you will be well served if enrolled in one, but you will want to be sure there is no more than a 10:1 student:teacher ratio in whatever class you take. If you are able to have the 1: 1 ratio of a tutor, the tutor will focus on improving your particular areas of challenge and will help you devise strategies for the particular test you are taking. And - something to share with your parents — because you will get one-on-one attention, you can get more done in fewer sessions, so it may not even end up being more expensive than a class.

Take and retake. Since there is no penalty for a low score following a high one, I advise kids to take the tests as often as they can. While some colleges will simply consider your best overall score, others will look at a "superscore," a compilation of your best scores across all the tests. Some of my students will even retake a test and just do the single section they want to improve, leaving the rest of the test blank.

Additional Organization

No matter what type of learners we are, we humans are still fundamentally visual creatures. Visual aids help us make sense of our worlds, even for those of us who are auditory or tactile learners.

And so I recommend helping your child color-code all of his notes - and, in fact, all of his materials -by subject. Your child will quickly come to think of all math materials as being in his blue binder, all Language Arts being in red, all science in green, etc. Life is always easier when you're organized!

Many classroom teachers use this sort of color- coding method, so make sure you are aligned with any system that's being used at school.

I also advise a written checklist, posted by the front door. For younger children or children with learning issues, it is often helpful to post a picture alongside each item as well:

- Is my homework for all my subjects in my backpack?
- Is my homework tracker in my backpack?
- Is my lunch (or lunch money) in my backpack?
- Are my keys in my pocket (or wherever they are kept)?
- Do I need a hat/scarf/gloves/sweater today?
- What day of the week is it? If I have an after-school activity today, do I have what I need for that activity?
- Did I kiss my mom/dad/grandma goodbye? (OK, this one's optional, but it's on my son's checklist!)

If you put the checklist on a dry-erase board or print and laminate it, your child can use a dry-erase marker to check off the items as she does them.

Praise, Encouragement and Rewards

I can't stress enough how important it is to motivate your child steadily and regularly. Children get turned off to school when it's been hard for them - after all, who likes a constant reminder of his or her shortcomings? So while you're helping your child gain the homework and study skills outlined in this chapter and the last one, it is absolutely critical to praise every attempt and to congratulate every single forward step, no matter how small and halting.

Take an interest in what your child is learning (without offering up judgment!), and look for ways to apply his own interests to the subjects he's covering in school. If your child is passionate about his local sports team, you can look at his favorite players' stats together to reinforce what he's doing in math. If your child loves skiing, you not only can find books at the library that will reinforce her reading skills, but can even learn about physics together in the context of skiing (friction, etc. -just exactly how do you figure out what an Olympic skier's speed would be?). Your tween daughter's obsession with a particular boy-band can be used to encourage research and reading, even if she starts with magazine articles. Even a love of video games can be turned into an exploration of computer programming and robotics.

When your child reaches a goal or masters a skill, celebrate the achievement. This can be as simple as the whole family toasting the child at dinner, a special small dessert, or a secret lunchbox note. My son knows that a level up in reading means a big "Congratulations!", calls to the grandparents, and dinner out at the local diner (on a school night!) with mom and dad . . .and you can bet your boots he can't wait for his next assessment!

CHAPTER EIGHT

WHEN HE GOT THERE. WHAT DID HE SEE? THE YOUTH OF AMERICA ON ILP!

In the 1960s, the "youth of America," according to the musical Hair, turned for its moment of self-reflection to LSD. Today, they have a better option: the ILP, or Individualized Learning Plan.

It's time to take stock.

Now that we've taken a look at all the major factors that go into successful learning:

- understanding and making the most of your child's learning styles
- designing a homework routine that works for your family, and
- helping your child develop superhero study skills

…it's time to talk turkey.

The previous chapters may have inspired you to set up a Homework Zone and implement a schedule for your seventh grader, to shift learning methods to accommodate your second-grade auditory learner, or to practice note–taking with your high school freshman. It's possible that adjusting one or more aspect of your child's learning profile has already dramatically changed his school experience. If so, great! After reading this chapter in "Your Child's Best Self", you may decide the changes you've made are sufficient. (I do suggest that you read on in any case, because the concepts I will discuss here are relevant to your child even if you decide not to implement the actual plan. You're doing a lot already. Perhaps think of what I outline here as "extra credit.")

However, if the previous chapters have presented so many ideas that would benefit your child that your head is starting to spin, or if your child is still frustrated and struggling, or even if you and your child simply work better with a very structured guideline, then this chapter introduces a comprehensive approach to assessing your child's needs and planning for her success.

So, without further ado: parent, please meet ILP. An ILP, or Individualized Learning Plan, is exactly what it sounds like: A comprehensive plan for your individual child's learning. In a sense, an ILP pulls together everything I've written about in this section of the book and gives your child a great way to organize it all…and to grow from the experience.

> **The ILP is both a *process* and a *working document***
> **That guides your child's entire year of learning.**

Creating an ILP

The steps to creating an ILP are simple. Some schools, especially in grades 8-12, are already implementing an ILP process for all kids. But if not, don't panic! You can initiate and drive the process yourself – and it's easy! The ILP is often used by educators to guide middle school and high school students in planning for a future career, but if your child is in elementary school, that's ok, too; the ILP can be adapted for all ages.

You may have noticed that I called ILP a process *and* a document. The document is a working, adjustable product of the process. Here's the whole process in six simple steps, some of which you have already done! (Notice, chunking works for grownups, too.)

Step One: Establish Ownership

I actually think this simple step is the most important part of ILP. Even if you go through the whole ILP process and never end up reviewing the document again, the ownership conversation is worth the whole endeavor!

Your child must understand and embrace the idea that ultimately she – and only she – is responsible for her own future. She must willingly take ownership of her education. Remember the child in Chapter One who was working on her own education construction site throughout grades K-12? Same idea here. The fact that your child's decisions now will actually affect her future can be a huge revelation! Perceiving the future as a series of destinations in a journey she has already begun rather than a far-off and distinct time from the present can completely change the way a child sees her choices. Internalizing this concept is a very positive and empowering step. Children often feel hemmed in by the restrictions and requirements adults place on them. This is a moment of liberation: the child is in control.

> **The child takes ownership of the path to his or her future.**

Step Two: Form Your Team

The ILP is a collaborative process. Now that you and your child have established his ownership of the process, together you can discuss who will be on your team. Some typical team members are: teachers, guidance or career counselors, parents, therapists, coaches, extracurricular instructors, and special mentors. For an elementary school student, the classroom teacher is a key team member; for a high school student, a guidance counselor is definitely someone you'd want to include.

Step Three: Assess the Student's Strengths and Challenges

This step is quite straightforward. If you've been using this book to assess your child's progress, you will have completed much of this already. Check this list and delve into any item you may have missed:

- Gather all summative test results you have, for as many years as they are available;
- Gather all recent formative test results (you may need to ask your child's school or teachers to provide these);
- Determine your child's learning style or styles;
- Investigate your child's interests and special abilities (You can simply compile this list with your child, or, if you're having trouble, one helpful resource for this is the Interests and Abilities Map from parentdrivenschools.com: http://www.parentdrivenschools.com/docs/pds_iam_form.pdf);
- Your child's IEP or 504, if he has one (If IEP and 504 are a mystery to you, don't worry–You will find I discuss it in the next section, "When Your Child Needs Extra Help").

Taken together, all of this information should give you and your child a very clear, well-rounded picture of his or her learning preferences and current academic progress, as well as his or her educational and personal strengths and challenges.

You know where your child stands. And so does your child. That's a very powerful thing.

Step Four: Identify the Student's Goals

Grades K-7

For elementary (and for the most part, middle school) students, this step has a single primary focus: sit down with your child and a copy of the appropriate GLEs (Remember those grade level expectations we talked about in Chapter One?). If you live in a Common Core state, you can simply go to http://www.corestandards.org to find these. If not, go to your state's online education portal (every state has one!) to find them. Using the info you gathered in Step Three, compare your child's academic standing with the GLEs for his grade (for younger children, you'll have to "translate" and explain this to your child) and help him choose a range of attainable goals for the upcoming year. Record these in your child's ILP. Be sure to include interim goals along the way (just like chunking homework!). Once you have set academic goals, give your child time to consider whether there are artistic, personal, or social goals he or she would like to add to the list.

Grades 7-12

For highly motivated middle school and all high school students, this step is a bit more complex and can be time-consuming. It's time for your child to think specifically about her future:

- Identify Career goals
  Yes! I said it! Despite the obvious value of a liberal arts education, despite the fact that diversity of knowledge enriches the development of innovations; despite the fact that your child has

years ahead of him in which to decide what to do with his life, Nevertheless, identifying career goals now is a very good idea (but don't worry – I will also discuss below how to proceed if your child simply has no idea of the direction in which he'd like to go).

Of course, it is possible and even likely that over the course of the next decade your child's path will vary significantly from what he plans on now–that's ok. Regardless of shifts that will happen down the line, by the time they reach high school kids have quite a store of self-knowledge; they're already discovering that there are certain kinds of work they both excel at *and* enjoy. If your child's ILP work up to this step has been thorough, his understanding of self will help him choose a learning path that is a good fit for him and will serve him well – even if he changes gears along the way.

This step in the ILP process requires investigation and deliberation. Be patient. The work your child is doing here is important and builds character. This work is called Career Exploration.

Take a look at the graphic below, which divides some of the most common career choices according to best fit with personality type:

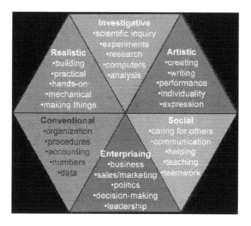

This graphic only includes generalizations of possible career choices, but it does give your child a framework in which to think about the type of job he or she might enjoy. If your child already has an idea of the general arena she'd like to work in, she can probably start with finding out more about careers that might interest her. The quote above about career exploration is from careeronestop.org, a free and very helpful resource provided by the U.S. Department of Labor. On careeronestop's video page, you and your child can view videos about over 500 different careers. Each video also tells you what kind of training, education, or certification your child would need to pursue that career.

But what if my child simply has no idea what she wants to do?

That's OK – Really! Despite her wealth of self-knowledge, your high school student may still have absolutely no idea what she would like to "be when she grows up".

The same resource listed above can help with that. Careeronestop also has videos that show many different skills and abilities and that explain which careers require those skills and abilities. Since your child has already pinpointed her strengths, this might be a good place to start:

http://www.careeronestop.org/Videos/SkillandAbilityVideos/skill-and-ability-videos.aspx

Some high school students have known since third grade that they want to be bakers, lawyers, or shoe manufacturers. Great! If your child is one such student, encourage him or her to use the resources above to learn more about his chosen career. Hopefully, he will discover that his personal strengths and abilities are well suited to the job, and that the training required is exciting to him. Doing a check like this will make sure that the single-minded student has a realistic idea of the requirements and lifestyle related to the chosen career.

- Identify academic goals necessary to those career goals
  While identifying his career goals, your child has also probably garnered some idea of the preparation necessary to achieving his goal. He may now know that after high school he will be heading for a vocational school, for college, or directly to a job search or internship application. What he needs to chart out in his ILP is his academic pathway through the current or upcoming school year, heading toward that milestone. The guidance counselor will be especially helpful with this.

- Include Related Non-academic Goals
  Once you have set academic goals, give your child time to consider whether there are artistic, personal, or social goals he could pursue that might affect his success in achieving his chosen career goal.

Step Five: Set a Plan for the School Year

Now your child gets to devise her own plan to achieve the goals she has set for herself, turning to her team members (including you, the parent) for guidance. Ideally, this discussion will take place at a meeting with all team members present.

Using her knowledge of her own best work and study practices, her abilities, talents, and challenges, and drawing upon the collective wisdom of her team members, your child will develop and record in her ILP a detailed plan of action.

For students of all ages, the plan should include:

- Any changes or adjustments that will be made in the classroom in light of learning styles, social-emotional issues, medical situations, etc.;
- Additional services that will be provided at school, if any, in light of the info being reviewed;

- Any changes or adjustments that will be made at home, including homework process or schedule and any contract that has or will be agreed to between the student and the parent or guardian;
- Supplemental work that will be done at home in order to catch up on particular skills or concepts;
- Outside resources that will be sought. These may include: private tutoring, occupational or social/emotional therapies, mentoring, extracurricular activities that support the child's needs and talents, or tutoring services such as Sylvan or Kumon (I'll discuss these further either in the next chapter and the following section of the book);
- Incentives or reward systems that will be put into place at school or at home, or both.

For eighth graders and high school students, the plan should also include:

- Projected scheduling of courses beneficial or necessary to the chosen career path;
- Special courses or tutoring to be arranged in preparation of career-oriented standardized testing.
- Extracurricular activities that support the child's career goal.

Step Six: Schedule Review and Revision

The ILP team should set dates on which it will review progress; these dates are recorded in the ILP and in the child's calendar. As the review dates come up, review all relevant materials (such as recent formative testing results) and if necessary adjust the ILP.

Our Child's Tutoring Service Gave Him an ILP–Isn't That Good Enough?

The term ILP can be used several different ways; although it can refer to an overall goal-oriented education plan like the one we've discussed in this chapter, many online and bricks-and-mortar tutoring services create what they refer to as an "ILP" based on a diagnostic assessment; this "ILP" is not about the child as a whole, but, rather, refers only to a very specific, detailed set of skills or standards the child has to master in order to move to the next grade level. An "ILP" of this kind can be very helpful because it identifies specific skill gaps you and your child can address in the more comprehensive ILP you're developing at home.

What if the school pre-empts my plan to introduce ILP?

You may find that your state, school district or school has a standard form it uses for ILP. Most often these are used beginning in 8th or 9th grade and are more narrowly defined. They may leave out a few or many of the steps above. That's ok! Your child may find that the ILP provided by the school meets his needs. If not, you and he should not hesitate to contact the team members and ask to add to the ILP, giving the team a more holistic view of your child's profile, goals and progress. If the school system's ILP process is not flexible and you feel your child would benefit from creating a separate document, it's a great idea to support him in this endeavor. Maybe your ILP (Home Edition) team will include your child, you, an outside tutor and his guitar teacher–that's OK, too. Let your child lead the way.

CHAPTER NINE

SOMETHING'S STILL IN THE WAY... SOME COMMON OBSTACLES TO ACADEMIC SUCCESS

We adults forget how difficult it can be to be a kid. I know, I know – you're thinking, "being an adult's no picnic, with bills to pay, clocks to punch…" but think back to the experience of being a child: First of all, kids have so much catch-up learning to do to understand what's going on around them in this bewildering world and to develop the analytical skills to interact within it. They are also largely powerless to control their lives, a fact that just adds to their frustration and stress. And the expectations heaped upon them – most notably at school – can be beyond their capacity to deliver upon, for many, many reasons, some of which I've already addressed.

At this point, you've read enough to know that when a parent comes to me because his child is not performing well in school, I look at the data to see what I can glean about the areas of challenge for the child. I also analyze the child's learning style and make tweaks to the child's homework routines and study habits. And I ascertain, as I will discuss in the next section of the book, what level of intervention would best serve the child. But just as a detective can sometimes overlook the most obvious clue, sometimes the obstacle to the child's learning is an additional factor that is still out there and is staring me – or the child – right in the face.

Sometimes the factor is external; sometimes it is within the child himself. It's beyond the scope of this book to give a comprehensive list or to go into great depth on each, but let's look at some of the most common obstacles to academic success apart from poor study skills or homework habits, a learning style that differs from the teacher's teaching style, and/or any outright learning difference such as dyslexia. And hopefully the list here will trigger additional ideas for you that may be factors for your particular child.

CIRCUMSTANCES OF YOUR CHILD'S LIFE

…may be creating stress that prevents her from being able to focus in school. Here are a few examples:

Bullying:

Your child may say little about his school day. Or he may deliver whole monologues about what his class is doing in science lab, in detail that makes you go cross-eyed. Either way, you may have no idea that your child is being bullied. Despite a concerted push by schools to implement bullying awareness programs and anti-bullying policies, bullying is still a terrible fact of school life for many of our children. It causes far-ranging negative effects in victims from low self-esteem to anxiety to depression.

And a team of UCLA psychologists studying the effects of bullying on academic performance showed in a 2010 study that victims of bullying performed not just more poorly but *significantly* more poorly academically than their peers who weren't bullied. In fact, being a victim of bullying and low academic performance "are *frequently* linked," [italics added] according to Jaana Juvonen, the UCLA professor of psychology who was the lead author of the study. Frequently linked. As the study discusses and observations by scores of educators bears out, bullied children are more afraid to participate in class for fear of being further targeted for speaking, and their lack of classroom participation, their low self-esteem, their anxiety about being bullied (which preoccupies their minds), and their depression all conspire against their doing well academically. When unaware of the bullying, teachers often mistake these students' low participation for lack of aptitude, interest or effort. Bullied students, ashamed of being outcasts, convinced that nobody cares anyway, and/or afraid of reprisal from their tormentors, are loath to tell anyone that they are being bullied, which makes your job as parent-detective all the harder, I know. And so I've listed many of the signals experts look to as indications that your child may be a victim of bullying:

- A change, whether sudden or gradual, in your child's affect – your child is withdrawn and sullen, sad, depressed, or angry without seeming cause;
- Bedwetting in an older child, or, for children of any age, difficulty sleeping and/or increased nightmares;
- Unexplained loss of his possessions or lunch money;
- Unexplained marks, bruises or cuts (or the unexplained wearing of long-sleeved shirts, if she's covering them up);
- Fears of riding the school bus or, in general, of being away from parent(s);
- Your child now regularly gets home from school extra-hungry (a sign that his lunch money is being stolen) or badly needing to use the restroom (an indication that she's afraid to use the restrooms at school, since restrooms are often bullies' favorite bullying spots);
- Frequent stomach aches, headaches or other ailments frequently related to stress;
- A sudden loss of friends or withdrawal from a formerly enjoyed activity;
- Your child's response to "how was your day," is an evasive one such as "kids were all kinda messing around."
- A marked decrease in self-esteem;
- Your child begins speaking of feeling lonely and/or hopeless, or speaks about suicide.

When you ask questions of your child, watch her reaction – often what she *doesn't* say speaks more loudly than what she does say. Also, your child's close friend(s) may be a good source of information when your child is not being forthcoming. Remember, children frequently won't speak up about being bullied for fear of repercussions from their bulliers. Whether you get the "smoking gun" proof or not, if you suspect bullying you should speak with your child's teachers and administrators right away. And you should praise your child for speaking with you openly about it if he does, and reassure your child that you believe him, that there is nothing to be ashamed of, and that you and he are a team, and you will be there for him and will take swift action with him and his school and, if necessary, with law enforcement, to stop the bullying.

Cyber-bullying is a possible source of anxiety as well; at first only found amongst middle- and high-schoolers, this form of bullying is on the rise and has now even reared its ugly head in elementary schools. Another of Juvonen's recent studies showed that nearly three in four teenagers experienced at least one incident of cyber-bullying in the 12-month study period – That's almost 75% of kids in the study! Only one in ten of these reported the incident to a parent or other adult. If your child is addicted to or even just dipping her toes into social networking, make sure you are involved.

Sibling Stress

You always fought with your siblings growing up. Everyone did. You chalk it up to the old adage, "kids will be kids." But sometimes the stress surrounding sibling strife can weigh heavily on a particular child. His older sibling's treatment of him may actually rise to the level of bullying, whether physical or emotional, he may feel unsafe in his own home, his self-esteem may plummet, and he may experience chronic stress. If sibling relations are strained in your home, please don't write off the possible effects on any one – or all – of your children. There are many ways to create greater accord between siblings, usually requiring both rewards and incentives for the behaviors you want and consequences for those behaviors you don't. It's important to be clear and specific about your expectations in advance, and then watch carefully and follow through with the rewards (along with great heapings of PRAISE!) and consequences you laid out. If your child's grades were suffering due to sibling stress, you'll have the satisfaction of knowing that you've helped your child in school AND have helped shape your children's relationship with each other for the rest of their days. Nice.

Changes at Home

Children rely upon consistency in their home life, and they are often fazed by changes at home, even good ones such as the birth of a new sibling or a move to a bigger home. And when a child is experiencing stress, her schoolwork invariably suffers. So if your child's academic performance has taken a sudden downturn, stop and ask yourself if anything at home has changed: Your child may be reacting adversely to positive changes such as those I just mentioned above, or to more difficult ones, such as your separation from her other parent, or from the death of a family member or close friend, whether a parent, sibling, grandparent, beloved uncle, neighbor, or even a pet. Be careful not to dismiss possible causes of distress: the rearranging of furniture in the living room, the swapping of your child's bedroom for the larger one vacated by her older, college-bound sibling, or the death of a hermit crab might seem minor to you, but to your child, these can take on great import and cause her grades to plummet.

Challenges in the Community

Let's face it, most of us don't live in gated communities. Neighborhoods can be rough. And even in the most idyllic locale, an event can take place that affects a whole neighborhood or community and causes anxiety in everyone…including its youngest members. One young girl I know lost her home and found herself and her family in a shelter that couldn't afford to launder sheets, so there were none on the beds. Another I know hears gunshots and sirens routinely at night. A California fire that wiped out three houses caused anxiety in countless children who live nearby, though their homes were unscathed. Many children in LA, where I'm from, live in fear of earthquakes, having experienced them firsthand. Please know that your children are astute and observant, and they know more than you know that they know. And the stress caused by challenges in the community can adversely affect your children's ability to focus on their schoolwork.

As with bullying, your child may not mention what is plaguing his thoughts, and detective work may be needed. If your community might be a cause of your child's challenges in school, I would recommend speaking candidly with your child's guidance counselor or school psychologist and suggesting that recent events or the ongoing dangers of your neighborhood may be posing a threat to your child's ability to focus in school.

PHYSICAL ISSUES

Your child's academic performance may be adversely impacted by physical issues. Topping this list are HUNGER and INADEQUATE SLEEP.

Hunger

Hunger in the US is a problem that affects fully one in four children, a fact I am shocked and saddened to report to you. Parents are working as hard as they can and still not managing to put enough food on the table each day to feed their children. Many families live in "food deserts" where wholesome and nutritious food is hard to come by, or the food is there, but parents find themselves needing to buy food with greater additives, preservatives and fillers and less nutritional value in order to make that dollar stretch.

It pains me to see how many children I work with rely on the free lunch they receive at school – for some, it is their only meal of the day. In the film *A Place at the Table*, eleven-year old Rosie describes how her stomach aches from hunger, and how, as she listens to her teacher, she starts to imagine the young woman morphing into a giant banana, the other students around her becoming apples and pears. Rosie would be a much better student if she could just focus on her teacher's lecture rather than her grumbling stomach. If you are a parent struggling to feed your child, I honor you for all you're doing to try to make ends meet; these are hard times. If your child's school participates in the federal School Breakfast Program or a state or city school breakfast program, try to get your child there in time. I realize that it's difficult for working parents to get their kids to school early, but the effort will pay off. Studies consistently show that children who eat breakfast get better grades and are 20% more likely to graduate from high school later on. If you are a parent whose paycheck can cover nutritional meals all month long, I urge you to take a hard look at what your child is eating, and see where you can replace junk food with whole food. Make sure your child has a good breakfast before heading off to school – if you don't feed that body, the brain will not be primed and ready to focus.

Inadequate Sleep

Good sleep is critical to your child's success in school – it's not only essential for growth, it fosters better alertness in the moment and memory in the long run. Performance improves when students get enough sleep; studies show that college students who get adequate sleep tend to get a full grade higher in a given course than those who are under-slept.

How much sleep is enough? Here's what doctors recommend, by age:

- 3-6 year olds: 10-12 hours per day;
- 7-12 year olds: 10-11 hours per day;
- 12-18 year olds: 8-9 hours per day.

Few students get enough sleep. I know your child has a lot of homework, and, perhaps, many extracurricular activities as well. This is why I urge you to create a schedule of your child's week that lays out when he is to do his homework, to ensure he has all the supplies he needs, and to limit distractions (see Chapter Five: HOMEWORK HAPPINESS). You'd be surprised at how much more efficient your child will be…which means that he will be finished sooner…which will mean he can go to sleep earlier. And don't think that your teenager can stay up until all hours of the night doing homework while also on social media (which makes the homework take exponentially longer), and then catch up on her *zzzzzs* on the weekend. Sleeping 'til 1 PM on Saturday and Sunday just throws off her circadian rhythms, which just makes getting up early from Monday through Friday that much more difficult.

There are other physical issues that can adversely affect your child's performance in school:

Vision Challenges (both focal and ambient)

Vision is the primary sense we humans rely on to get around, so it goes without saying that if there is trouble with your child's vision, there will be trouble with school. But ruling out some aspect of vision as the culprit in a child's struggles at school is not as easy as you might think, as you will see.

80% of what children learn is processed through their eyes.

Vision 1.0

Most people are only aware of one aspect of their vision, the one for which they are typically tested by the optometrist. The optometrist tests your **visual acuity**, or the sharpness of the image you see. She is checking for refractive problems such as nearsightedness (blurry vision far away), farsightedness (blurry vision close to you), or astigmatism (straight lines appearing bent or wavy). Most refractive errors can easily be corrected with glasses or contact lenses. The optometrist is also checking for eye-turning (strabismus) and lazy eye (amblyopia), conditions that can be treated with corrective lenses, an eye patch, eye exercises, and/or surgery, and must be treated early to avoid permanent vision loss.

Well, my child is checked yearly at her annual visit, and also in a quick test at school. She was checked a few months ago, so that can't be the problem...

Yes, your child is probably checked once a year by her pediatrician or her school or both, and that's a good thing. However, children's vision can change *very* quickly, especially during a growth spurt. I worked with one second-grader whose vision had been checked at his annual physical right before the start of school. Over the next three months, his schoolwork began to slide, and by Thanksgiving the teacher asked to meet with his parents, who brought me along. It turned out that Pavel had gone through a huge growth spurt that fall, and he now needed glasses to see the smart board and the white board his teacher used for most of her lessons. Pavel had never had a problem with his vision before, and at age seven wasn't even aware that what he saw was unusual or that he should tell an adult about it.

So as you see, it can be slightly tricky to keep right on top of children's eye health and visual acuity. But all in all, you know what to look for and it's not too confusing.

Beyond All That – Vision 1.1, 1.2, 1.3...

But you might be surprised to learn that there are other ways that vision problems can impede your child's learning, and these can sometimes elude detection for a while. In addition to being able to see sharply, in order to use our vision in a learning environment

- our eyes must function well in practice (i.e., when asked to track a line of text, or quickly change focus from one distance to the next), and
- our brains must quickly and efficiently process what they see.

Just as Pavel didn't realize his blurry vision meant he needed glasses, children who experience differences *in the way their brains process what they see and the way their eyes function when challenged* may not realize that what they experience is any different than what anyone else is experiencing. Therefore it's your job to be the sleuth.

These signs might indicate that your child's eyes are not functioning up to par:

- He rubs, closes, or covers one eye;
- He often loses his place when reading, or persists in using his finger as a guide;
- He often re-reads the same line or skips lines while reading;
- He complains of eyestrain or headache;
- His attention span is short when reading or studying;
- He says things like, "The words keep moving around," "The letters are scrambled," "The words keep getting blurry," or "The words are all jumping around on the page."
- He has trouble copying from the board in class;
- He lays his head down on the book or holds the book very close to his face, even though he is not nearsighted;
- He has good decoding skills but poor comprehension.

And all of the above, in addition to the signs below, could be signs that your child is struggling with processing what she sees:

- She has trouble picking out specific items or information on a page;
- She has trouble seeing the difference between two similar letters or shapes;
- She has trouble when using a separate answer sheet (such as with standardized tests);
- She frequently reverses or misreads numbers and words.

If your child regularly experiences or exhibits more than one or two of the signs above, make an appointment with a developmental optometrist (also known as a behavioral optometrist or sometimes a neuro-optometrist), a specialist who can diagnose the problem and prescribe treatment.

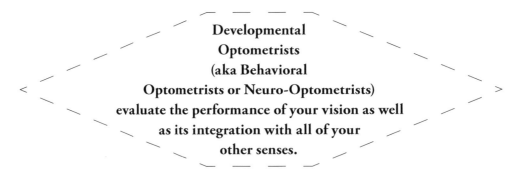

Developmental Optometrists (aka Behavioral Optometrists or Neuro-Optometrists) evaluate the performance of your vision as well as its integration with all of your other senses.

Most often, treatment for these issues involves either vision therapy to strengthen and retrain the eye muscles or visual processing activities with an occupational therapist––or both. It may also involve glasses with special lenses or glasses with prisms, either for everyday use or just for use during therapy. You can visit http://pavevision.org/find-a-doctor/ to find a developmental optometrist near you.

> **If your child experiences more than one or two of the signs listed in this section, please seek help. Vision problems that affect learning will not 'just go away'. Some of these issues can be cured, but only with vision therapy; others are learning challenges that require practice with an occupational therapist and learned strategies in order to ease your child's struggles and make reading and writing––and academic success!––possible.**

Color Blindness

Color blindness, or color vision deficiency, is an inherited trait that (for now) can't be corrected. It's not considered a learning difference, as it doesn't really affect a child developmentally. It's important to be aware, though, that color blindness can cause difficulty in the classroom. In pre-K and Kindergarten, color-matching and color identification are popular activities. Many early-grade classrooms use color-coding on a daily basis as a tool for learning and organization and might mistake your child's color blindness for failure to understand a concept. Teachers of older children don't give a thought to using color-coded assignments. If your child is color blind, make sure you alert his teacher so she can accommodate him in her classroom systems and please read Chapter Eleven to learn how you can secure classroom accommodations that will safeguard your child's learning.

Hearing and Auditory Processing Challenges

Hearing

Obviously, your child's hearing should be checked regularly. Faulty hearing is frequently missed, causing a child to be seen as unfocused, disinterested or even less intelligent than he actually is.

Poor Auditory Processing

This is similar to hearing, but is a challenge of the vestibular system and the central nervous system rather than the ear itself. When a child has poor auditory processing, she can hear what is being said but not process the individual words. Long strings of words, uttered too quickly, are simply not understood. I asked my friend's five-year old, a very bright boy, "What do you put on your finger when you get a boo-boo?" Jayden knows you put a band-aid on a boo-boo and has a whole collection of band-aids with various favorite cartoon characters on them. But the only words he actually processed were "…you get a boo-boo?" Deeply concerned, he asked, "You got a boo-boo? Where? You OK?"

Children with auditory processing issues become anxious children as well, since they realize they've been spoken to and are expected to reply, but they don't know what was said and what to answer. The pressure to answer correctly can be too much to bear, and they may also withdraw. Furthermore, teachers will frequently misconstrue the child's hesitance: often quite bright, like little Jayden, they are often labeled as slow (as I mentioned about children with hearing loss) and put on an altogether incorrect academic track. If you suspect auditory processing disorder, please make sure to go to an audiologist who knows how to test for it (not all do) and ask that this be done.

Sensory Processing Disorder

This is harder to explain than all of the above put together. Every piece of information you have ever received about the world in which you live has come to you through one or more of your senses. Lemons are sour, roses smell rosey, the leaves on trees in summer are usually various shades of green, snow is cold, a puppy's nose is cold and wet, but his ears are velvety. We listen to our teachers (hearing), we read books (vision)…everything we learn comes to us through our senses.

We take it for granted that stimuli will come through our senses the same every time. I turn the water dial in my shower to the same spot each morning, and the water is the temperature I like it to be. In fact, however, the stimuli do vary. There are certain days – and even certain times of day – when sounds will simply seem louder, for example. How many of you have ever found yourselves saying, "Kids, please keep it down until I've had my morning coffee?" I rest my case. But while the response to sensory stimuli are somewhat variable for everyone, for most of us these responses are still fairly reliably consistent and we just don't give them a thought.

For many children, however (some studies say one in twenty, others say the number is as high as one in six), sensory stimuli do not come through their sensory systems reliably at all. One sense may be unreliable, or more than one, or all. Sounds that don't bother most people may be experienced as piercingly loud, lights painfully bright, touch painfully acute. The hum of a fluorescent light may drive them to distraction. Or any of the sensory stimuli may be coming in too softly. Some children are hence "sensory-seekers" while other are "sensory avoiders," and some are both. One child I knew could barely perceive touch and didn't react when accidently injured or burned. Imagine how dangerous this could be if infection set in. Many children I've worked with are traumatized by fire drills at school, and the school administrators don't understand that the children are actually experiencing pain, not just the fear of an unexpected noise. The chronic experience of extremes in sensory response to input form one or more of the senses is currently referred to as Sensory Processing Disorder (SPD, formerly called "Sensory Integration Dysfunction"). I say "currently referred to" because the medical community has not come to consensus on this issue and – much to the dismay of doctors and occupational therapists – there is no diagnosis code for it, which causes practitioners to use related but inaccurate codes to get their patients the services they need.

And that's just the beginning of the challenges a parent faces with SPD. Here's another: I know you've learned about the five senses of sight, hearing, taste, smell and touch through which we take in external stimuli, but in fact we have two more innate senses we don't usually learn about…unless they're not functioning well: our vestibular system, through which we experience the effect of gravity on us and our proprioceptive system, through which we receive feedback from our muscles and joints. Both help us understand where we are in space.

Children with under-responsive vestibular systems can't put their hands out to break a fall because they have no idea which direction is up and which way they're falling. Children with under-responsive proprioception rub up against walls and other people in order to get the input about where their bodies end and space begins that other children receive from the air around them. Imagine how these children are mislabeled as having behavioral problems. Likewise, the child who is over-responsive to proprioceptive or tactile input, who seems to over-react if another child merely touches him. He is perceived as aggressive and is disciplined, when, in fact, he is acting appropriately protective of himself…in the context of his perception of the world around him. An understanding teacher will always place this child at the front or back of a line, to diminish by 50% his likelihood of being bumped by a classmate. Sensory Processing Disorder is frequently mislabeled as ADHD, when, in fact, the children in question need regularly-scheduled motion breaks to reset their sensory systems. How a particular child with SPD presents depends on which senses are impacted, and whether the senses in question tend to be under- or over-responsive. SPD is frequently called "the hidden disability" because it is so rarely recognized in a child for what it is. As a result:

- The child is often uncoordinated, unable to perform well in sports and other motor activities;
- The child is often ostracized by other children;
- The child is aware of her inability to perform tasks that come readily to other children;
- The child is frequently unable to perform in school and is berated for "not trying harder";
- The child is frequently disciplined for what is actually a manifestation of her SPD;
- Having been mislabeled a behavior problem for so long (most especially the sensory-seekers), the child grows into an adolescent who decides "I've been called 'bad' for so long that I might as well *be* bad," and becomes a true behavioral problem;
- For any or all of the above reasons, the child suffers low self-esteem and depression.

I could go on and on. The bottom line is that if you read this and suspect that your child's sensory system (or some aspect thereof) might be "out of sync" (to quote the title of a great book on the subject, *The Out-of-Sync Child*, by Carol Stock Kranowitz), you might want to look further at Ms. Kranowitz's book plus you might want to ask your Department of Ed for an Occupational Therapy evaluation by an occupational therapist well-versed in Sensory Integration and SPD. Occupational Therapy can do wonders for a child with SPD. As a result of SPD, my friend's son Jake could not motor-plan enough to point his finger until he was twenty-seven months old, something most babies do between eight and ten months of age. At age ten, though, you should hear Jake play the piano.

EMOTIONAL OBSTACLES

Anxiety

First of all, all of the above can cause the primary emotional obstacle I'll discuss: anxiety. Anxiety can exist on its own, as a biochemical disorder, or it can arise from any of the obstacles to learning that I've written about above, or it can be the result both of brain chemistry AND any of the obstacles to learning I've mentioned.

Whatever has caused anxiety to take root in your child, when it does so it can highjack her thoughts, can interfere with participation in classroom or extracurricular activities, and can be exhausting. Please do not dismiss signs of anxiety in your child, or tell her "there's nothing to feel anxious about," or expect her to "just get over it." She can't do so on her own.

Signs of anxiety include:

- Constant worrying, about anything and everything;
- Avoidance of situations or places due to fearfulness of them;
- A reluctance to separate from you;

- Complaints of headaches or stomach aches;
- Full-blown panic attacks (these are unmistakable).

The child often feels great anxiety in part because she feels a lack of control over whatever she perceives is threatening her. Giving her ways to assert some control over her circumstances can be quite effective, even if it is not the whole solution.

If you see signs of anxiety in your child, please speak with her school psychologist right away. There may be external factors such as bullying to help her address and resolve, or the cause may be biological, in which case there are remedies both psychopharmacological, such as anti-anxiety medications, and psychological, such as cognitive-behavioral techniques that are quite effective with anxiety. With the help of experts, you can determine what you think is the best course of action for your particular child. Whatever the cause, she will need the reassurance of the adults in her life that you are all going to help her feel better.

Depression

Children of any age can suffer from depression. As with anxiety, the causes can be external or internal/biological.

Some signs of depression in children include:

- Decreased interest in activities your child previously enjoyed (but hasn't "grown out of");
- Self-isolation, and the preference to be alone rather than engage socially;
- Increased irritability or hostility;
- Seemingly low energy and/or an increase in the desire to sleep;
- A decrease in expressiveness, a marked decrease in excitement, and lower energy;
- The expression of feelings of hopelessness;
- Signs or the expression of suicidal thoughts.

As with anxiety, if you suspect your child is depressed, please seek help pronto! You can always start with the school psychologist. There is much that can be done to alleviate depression, and, as with anxiety, there is no reason for your child to be suffering when help is available to him.

Anger

Oh, my, such a hard one. Adolescents in particular tend to express anger, and it's hard to know whether it's merely age-appropriate venting or a problem requiring intervention. Anger is often an appropriate and healthy response to a given situation…but there are many people who struggle with anger that's out of control. In a child or teen, the anger can be turned outward towards others or inward towards herself. Cutting is an example of anger turned toward the self. Anger in children can cause them to hurt themselves or others and it can shut them down and prevent their engagement in learning.

As with the other emotional challenges I've discussed, I would first turn to the school psychologist as a resource, and, if this isn't possible, find another child psychologist to work with. I would strive to ascertain if there is something happening in the child's life that is prompting an anger response and assure your child you are there to help her. Whether you are able to pinpoint an external cause of the anger or not, teaching anger management can be highly effective. Often, the child is ultimately outright relieved to be given the tools to harness and feel more in control of this powerful emotion.

In conclusion

Your child's grades and test scores may indicate that something is amiss at school even though neither you nor his teachers can pinpoint any of the obstacles I've discussed. You may have given your best effort in every one of the areas I've presented in this book and still not seen improvement. If that situation rings a bell, think through the topics I've covered here, and be candid with yourself – Sometimes the fear of discovering there really is something hurting our children clouds our vision and blinds us to situations we badly need to face. If you have been thorough in your survey and honest with yourself, then there may be another piece of the puzzle that is missing – such as an undetected learning difference – and you may need some professional help to sort out the cause or causes of the trouble and set your child back on the road to happiness and success.

In the next section, "When Your Child Needs Extra Help", I will lay out all the interventions that are available to your child, in a clear and simple progression from the least restrictive (the comprehensive school 'safety net' policy that is designed to catch a child at the very beginning of his need for intervention), all the way through the series of options that lead to the need for the most involved solution (protection under the Individuals with Disabilities Education Act (IDEA) through the implementation of an Individualized Education Plan or IEP). If the many strategies and concepts I've presented thus far have still left you at loose ends with regard to your child's progress in school, I urge you to read on.

SECTION THREE

WHEN YOUR CHILD NEEDS EXTRA HELP

We've traveled a long way together since we first met on Page One.

Having read Section One, you now have a solid working knowledge of what happens in the classroom – at every grade level – and why, and you know that your child's teachers are all, in effect, scientists, weighing and measuring your child's progress in a variety of ways on a daily basis. By this point, you have studied all the blueprints for that educational edifice I described your child building back in Chapter One.

Having read Section Two, you are now toting a tool belt of your own and are ready to step in as site manager, making sure your child is equipped to build that building up to code.

But some of our builders need additional and/or different equipment, or they might need extra help in utilizing the same tools as their peers. If you're still reading this book, your child might be one of these terrific yet challenged builders. This section will lay out what schools do to flag these builders and help them, and what else you might do when those steps are not enough.

If your child is struggling in school right now and you know that your child needs more than the resources set out in Section Two, you may be feeling overwhelmed, I know. Just take this Section one step at a time.

I'll walk you through:

- How schools keep students from falling behind and help them catch up if they do anyway;
- How you can help keep your child on track or bring your child back up to speed outside of school hours;
- How to get accommodations and modifications in the classroom and/or for testing when your child needs them; and
- How to secure special education services and classroom placements when your child needs those.

You'll gain a sense of what you can do to build the scaffolding your child needs to build that building.

CHAPTER TEN

RTI: THE SCHOOL SAFETY NET

I'm excited for you to read this chapter – I'm eager for you to know about **"Response to Intervention"** (RTI). First of all, it's data driven, and, as you know by now, I love data. But secondly and more to the point, as a parent you will find it useful to know about RTI. If you know about it, you can help ensure that it is being implemented in your child's classroom, to his benefit.

And therein lies the beauty of RTI: As a parent, your simply knowing that RTI exists and understanding what it is is more important than your knowing all the ins and outs of how it works. Thus, in this chapter I'll give you an overview of what RTI is and a brief explanation of how it's implemented, as well as some tips for parent involvement, and I will spare you the minutiae that I'd include were I writing this book for education practitioners.

Remember Nyla? Social, well-liked Nyla who was in danger of not graduating with her high school class? Had Nyla's mom known about RTI and been able to ask her daughter's teachers about it, perhaps she could have insisted that they flag Nyla for help under this system sooner than they ultimately did...

The Quick Backstory

Very, very briefly, the Individuals with Disabilities Education Act (IDEA), which I mentioned in Chapter Two, codifies how states and public agencies are supposed to provide early intervention, special education and related services to children with special needs. But there was a problem inherent in the system prior to 2004, when IDEA was reauthorized: as it stood until then, the system seemed to set up what educators now call a "wait to fail" approach. In other words, students weren't getting flagged to receive help until they were already so far behind as to qualify for special education. Also, schools were supposed to take into consideration whether there was a significant discrepancy between a child's measured IQ and her performance in school. But what about the children whose learning differences are not so severe that they should wind up in a special education setting, or children without learning differences who might have been falling behind for other reasons? Until 2004, there was no standardized mechanism for observing their day-to-day success. What could be set up to help teachers notice when a given child needs assists...before that child is too far behind to catch back up to his peers?

Enter "Response to Intervention," or RTI for short. When IDEA was reauthorized in 2004, it contained a few new provisions. One of them provided for the implementation of RTI, a framework for early assessment and intervention intended to

1) enable educators to notice those instances in which children of all learning abilities are beginning to lag behind their classmates, and

2) provide intervention, at increasing degrees of intensity as needed, to get the majority of children back on track in general education and to direct towards special education only those children who really need to be there.

> **There was a problem inherent in the system prior to 2004, when IDEA was reauthorized: as it stood until then, the system seemed to set up what educators now call a "wait to fail" approach. In other words, students weren't getting flagged to receive help until they were already too far behind.**

A Quick Description of RTI

Imagine a classroom of, oh, let's say twenty-four fifth graders. Their teachers have looked over the end-of-year summative assessments (remember those from Chapter Three?) and have already noted that seven of the students had lower-than average scores in math and/or reading. The teachers are using teaching methods that are scientifically proven to be effective (more on that below). They are providing ongoing formative and benchmark assessments (remember *those* from Chapter Three?) to determine each student's response to the particular teaching methods being used and to flag any students who are not learning at a steady rate and/or at the same rate as the rest of the students. The seven students who seem to need extra help are given it, at increasing levels of intervention. At the start, all seven are given targeted interventions, often working at separate tables in the classroom. Each student's progress is carefully monitored throughout. Five seem to be responding well; the other two, however, prove to need more intensive interventions and are pulled aside for individual meetings with the teacher while the rest of the class completes other assignments. After a few weeks, one of the seven children still has not caught up to his peers in math, and is pulled out of class twice weekly to work with the school's math coach. Parents are kept in the loop and involved in the process. Six of the seven have caught up within an eight-week period. The seventh, though, hasn't caught up after receiving intensive interventions for most of that eight-week period. He is then referred for a comprehensive evaluation, to see if he might need either special accommodations or special education services.

The Components of RTI

Here are some of the key elements of RTI:

High quality, scientific, research-based instruction (SRBI). This basically means methods of teaching that have undergone scientifically based research and have had data collected on them to determine how effective they are, and which have, in fact, been shown to be effective instructional practices.

Universal Screening (School-wide or district-wide) of All Students in General Ed Classes. This means that all students get assessed to ascertain their skills and levels of knowledge. Yes, yours, too. This is the first step in the implementation of RTI.

Tiered Instruction, Increasing in Intensity. I will explain this in greater depth shortly. In brief, though, this means that those children flagged during the universal screening as being "at risk" will be given interventions at varying degrees of intensity and frequency of data collection (tiers) as needed, in order to help those children advance in the areas in which they are struggling.

Close Monitoring of All Student Progress. This is actually a scientifically based process, by which students' academic performance is frequently and carefully assessed to gauge the efficacy of the instruction (in other words, the student's *Response to Intervention*) and the gains the student is making. Based on the information the monitoring yields, adjustments to the tier of instruction can be made.

Communication with Parents and Parent Participation. This is an important aspect of RTI. From the time a student is flagged for intervention, parents are brought into the RTI process and their involvement is documented. They receive detailed information about the challenges facing their children, the intervention to be implemented and its frequency, and, then, the rate of progress observed. Parents' knowledge of their children and their collaboration in implementing learning strategies are seen as key to the success of the intervention.

Informed, Data-Based Decision-Making. The student performance data that is collected is analyzed so that the school can determine the effects of the intervention and what the student needs moving forward.

A Multi-Tiered Approach

Though there is no uniform single way in which RTI is carried out nationwide, it is generally implemented as a three-tiered model, so that's what I'm going to describe here:

Tier One. As noted above, all children in the general education classroom are given high-quality, scientific, research-based instruction and are screened. This tier is also referred to as "best practices." This tier is generally successful for about 90% of students.

Tier Two. Those learners whose assessments reveal that they are struggling are given more intensive instruction in small groups within the classroom, in order to speed up their rate of learning. These children are given both the same instruction as the rest of the class and additional targeted instruction aimed at the areas of learning in which they need extra help. They type of help is measured and tweaked as needed until each child has caught up to the rest of the class. Instruction is usually given by the classroom teachers, though they'll also sometimes receive instruction from additional educators. Somewhere from 5-10% of the students will require this level of instruction in order to catch back up to their peers.

Tier Three. If data being collected on Tier Two students shows that any are not making adequate progress despite the intervention, they will be given Tier Three interventions. At this tier, students receive intensive one-on-one tutoring and more frequent assessments of their progress. Classroom teachers and specialists provide the more intensive instruction. Only 1-5% of students tend to need Tier Three instruction.

Pull-Out vs. Push In

In prior years, Tier-Two and Tier-Three students had been pulled out of class for additional targeted instruction. Under Common Core recommendations, no student should be pulled out of class and miss core instruction in order to receive intensive supplemental instruction. Such supplemental instruction is supposed to happen within the classroom so that the student does not fall farther behind.

"RTI for Behavior": Positive Behavioral Interventions and Supports (PBIS)

The 1997 reauthorization of IDEA added language about a parallel evidence-based approach to supporting positive behavior in the classroom. I think I speak for all of us when I say that this was a good thing, since, obviously, a centered student in a calm classroom is a student who is ready for and receptive to learning.

Positive Behavioral Interventions and Supports (PBIS) is a problem-solving model intended to prevent unwanted behaviors. PBIS teaches and then reinforces desired behaviors rather than waiting for undesired behaviors to occur and then correcting them after they've happened. Recognizing, though, that not all children will be able to respond to the behavioral supports already in place in the classroom, PBIS offers increasing levels of support to those students who need it.

With PBIS, as with RTI:

- the universal behavioral plan for the classroom is evidence-based;
- all students' progress is monitored;
- there are tiers for students needing varying degrees of additional interventions;
- those interventions are evidence-based;
- the students' progress is monitored, and data collected (I love this!); and
- decisions regarding continued interventions are made based on the data collected.

Information gathered about those students who need additional behavioral support is used to determine, and then diminish or remove, the triggers to the negative behavior while adding what's needed to trigger more appropriate behavior in the classroom.

How You-The-Parents Can Be Involved

Here, finally, is the main course, the "meat and potatoes" of this chapter. You now understand what RTI is (and its behavioral counterpart, PBIS).

Recognizing that

- when schools and families collaborate, students win;
- different families have different ways of supporting their children's studies; and
- you, the parents, are the foremost experts on your own children,

the developers of RTI incorporated parent involvement into the RTI process.

RTI assumes that parents are already being informed and consulted by teachers. This may or may not be so across the board, but hopefully I've already given you plenty of suggestions in the preceding chapters for communicating with your child's teachers on an ongoing basis. With RTI, the partnership between educators and parents increases when a student is in need of Tier Two, and would increase further if the student was then assessed as needing Tier Three intervention.

If you think your child is struggling, be sure to be in touch with your child's teacher and speak candidly about whether recent assessments might be confirming your suspicions. If not, you should still explain why you've been worrying, so that you and your child's teacher can discuss the matter. If you were right, ask exactly what is being done. Your child's teacher should be outlining a plan that sounds like "Tier Two," above.

If your child is getting the additional interventions, some steps you can take to support your child's progress include:

- Check the "parent portal" or other means of school-parent communication;
- Ask for a daily form of communication if there isn't one in place;
- Meet regularly with your child's teacher(s) throughout the RTI process;
- Be sure to let your child know that you're "on her team," there to support her in whatever way she needs;
- In keeping with what I've written in Chapters Five and Six about homework and study skills, be sure you've set her up to succeed with homework and to know how to study in class and at home. Review her work with her to help her put those study habits in place; and,
- Find opportunities to read with your child. Even if your child is older, you can still find an article of interest to her to share together. As I've written repeatedly by now, the more you help your child love to read, the easier a time she'll have in school.

Ignorance is not Bliss

Never underestimate the power of parental knowledge! A client's son did not get the help he needed in math until I advised his mom to say to his teacher and the school's math coach, "I think he needs RTI." BOOM! She suddenly received a long email response to her concerns and an offer to meet in person within a few days. Now, we'll never know whether this was because she'd sparked a fear in the school of being accused of breaking the law, or whether the use of the term "RTI" signaled to the school the level of the mother's worry about her child. It doesn't matter: One way or another, her son got the help he needed.

You now know how your child's school can be monitoring your child's progress and working to catch your child up in areas where she might be slipping.

So. Let's suppose your child is slipping. And isn't catching up.

There are, in my mind, three levels of intervention, any one of which might be applicable to your child. From the least amount of intervention to the most, they are:

- **Private Tutoring/Off-Site Programs**. For the Typical Learner in a general ed classroom who is having trouble with a particular concept or subject, or for a special ed learner who is struggling with academic concepts and application of skills in addition to her other challenges. I am about to discuss this in Chapter 11;
- **"Section 504" Accommodations**. For the child who has a physical or mental disability that is impeding learning, but who can learn in a general education setting if the proper accommodations are in place. I will discuss this in Chapter 12.
- **An Individualized Education Program (IEP)**. For the child for whom accommodations in a general ed setting without supports such as therapies or counseling are not enough to level the playing field, who needs some level of special education supports and services in order to learn. I will discuss this in Chapter 13.

CHAPTER ELEVEN

WHEN YOUR CHILD NEEDS MORE THAN RTI: GETTING HELP OUTSIDE SCHOOL

It's pretty clear that RTI, as a theory, is a great idea, right? RTI is designed to catch each child's stumbling blocks early on and provide support before the child falls too far behind. And in many, many cases, it does. But no system is perfect, and there are times and situations in which RTI simply isn't enough. Maybe your child is benefitting from RTI, but progress is very slow; maybe you and your child's educators disagree about his needs and abilities, and your child has not been given the help you feel he needs; maybe his troubles stem from issues RTI doesn't address, such as poor study or organizational skills. If RTI has not brought your child up to speed, it's time to take next steps.

Should I Get My Child Extra Help?

I've heard this question countless times. Tutoring can be expensive, and it will definitely cut into your child's creative play time, which is just as essential to his development as his academics, so make sure this is something your child needs before you commit. The time to consider tutoring outside the school system is when you've exhausted all avenues; you've asked the questions, you've tried all other options, and you're not getting results.

"Which Kind of Tutoring Should We Choose?"

Many clients have come to me with questions about different kinds of tutoring, wanting to know which kind is best. My answer is always the same: every family's needs are different. The choice is completely subjective, so it really comes down to examining the options and choosing the one that is best for your family and your child.

In this chapter, I will introduce to you the different types of academic help available outside school, and will give you information about each that will help you decide which outside resource is right for your child.

Supplemental Education Services

Before we get into services you pay for out of pocket, you should know that if your child attends a Title 1 school, she may be eligible for outside tutoring that is paid for by the state. No Child Left Behind requires certain Title 1 schools to provide Supplemental Educational Services (known by educators as…say it with me: SES). If your child attends one of these schools and you qualify under your school district's criteria as 'low income', you should receive notice from the school that your child is eligible for SES.

SES consists of tutoring services offered by private companies, public institutions, or afterschool programs that have been pre-approved by the state. States are required to give parents a list of approved providers, and the list must include as many providers as possible—organized by school district—to ensure that parents and students have a wide variety of options to choose from. If your child is eligible for SES, your school or local department of education should have support services to help you decide which provider will be the best fit for your child's needs and learning style.

Your child is eligible for SES if your family is financially eligible and the school meets one of the following three criteria:

- in corrective action,
- in restructuring, or
- has not met Adequate Yearly Progress (known as—you guessed it—AYP) for two consecutive years.

If you believe your child meets these criteria but you have not been offered SES, contact your state education agency.

Out-of-Pocket (and a Few Free!) Tutoring Options

If your family does not qualify for SES or if you are not happy with the SES options available to your family, you have quite an array of choices to explore, encompassing a wide range of methodologies and costs. Each option has pros and cons, especially with regard to your specific child's needs, learning styles, strengths, and challenges. I've laid out your options below, starting with solutions that require the least parent involvement and working toward home-based and then parent-managed options.

Learning Centers

As a working mom, I get it that tutoring your own child is really hard—for so many reasons! By the time I get home from work and start to get dinner on the table, it's a real challenge to find the time to review my son's day at school and talk with him about his homework—never mind finding an additional 20 to 60 minutes for extra academic work. Even more important, I treasure the limited time I have to spend with my son, and of course I'd rather be outside tossing a Frisbee with him than forcing him to repeat his times tables! So it doesn't surprise me that many, many parents are looking for a one-stop, pre-fab solution to academic struggles. This is why on-site learning centers have become so popular, sprouting up across the country. For busy families with twenty-first century schedules, learning centers can be a very good answer.

The first thing you need to know is that most of the companies that provide on-site tutoring are franchised businesses, which means that they are individually owned and can vary in quality. So it's a good idea to get feedback from other parents about the particular branch you're considering before you decide to enroll. In large cities there may be more than one branch near you, so word of mouth can help you choose the branch that is the best fit for you.

"Which Learning Center is Best?"

That's the question I hear most often from parents who are considering enrolling their child in a learning center. What I tell them is that a good fit depends largely on your child's needs, temperament and learning style. Here's a list of the four largest companies, and a general idea of their strengths:

> **Do Your Research!**
>
> This section is meant to give you a general idea of the kinds of services that are out there. Of course, every franchise location is different, and very company changes over time, so these descriptions are not meant to steer your decision towards one company or another, but to help you think through the myriad options so that you can choose a solution that works best for your child and your family. Service and offerings may have changed since this writing, so do your footwork and ask questions before you sign on the dotted line!

Kumon

This international company originated in Japan and its strengths lie in discipline, traditional methods, and self-instruction. Children are assessed and each starts at his own level of competence (regardless of grade level) and progresses at his own speed through the levels, repeating sets of worksheets until competence in each skill is reached. The program requires attendance at the branch one or two times a week and completion of assigned work at home, which is expected to take 10 to 30 minutes each day.

Kumon's structure is staunchly linear, following a structure that is familiar to parents as what we knew as children. Addition of single digits is followed by addition of two digits; addition is followed by subtraction, which is followed by multiplication, and so on. Kumon's philosophy matches the idea I set out in Chapter One of your child's construction project perfectly. It will provide a rock solid base in math facts and algorithms, increasing your child's speed and accuracy, and allowing one skill to rest securely on the strength of the one before. In most schools today, however, children are following a spiraled curriculum (where material is covered in short units and revisited in increasingly complex ways over time) rather than a linear curriculum, due to the demands of the Common Core. Thus, if your child hits a unit on geometry and gets stuck, Kumon will not jump in and help him through the next few weeks; he will be assessed and start at his level of competency. If that level is multiplication, then geometry is way down the line, and by the time he gets to it, the math he's studying at school will have changed to fractions or units of measurement or algebraic thinking.

Kumon utilizes frequent timed tests and requires independent learning, two factors that will help prepare a child for the requirements–for better or worse–of public school instruction. If your child enjoys order and structure, thrives on routine and repetition, and works well on his own, Kumon will likely be a good fit. Because its main focus is on drills and worksheets, Kumon is a good place to turn if your child needs to work on mastering math facts. That is, however, unless your child processes material more slowly, in which case Kumon's timed tests will never reflect what he actually knows. I suggest that if your child is a strongly kinesthetic and/or auditory learner, you try to convince the manager of the branch you are considering to allow you child a trial period, so you can be sure he can handle the time spent sitting still and working alone quietly. If your child is already struggling to complete schoolwork in the time available, you will have to plan ahead for fitting the additional 30 minutes per day into his schedule.

Sylvan Learning Centers and Huntington

Sylvan and Huntington are two other large franchise-structured businesses, but their model is much different from Kumon. Sylvan uses small-group instruction, so your child will most likely work with a tutor and two other children. Huntington uses either one-to-one instruction, or small-group instruction in groups of four. Both of these companies (and a few smaller companies like them) are able to provide instruction in a wide range of subjects as well as study skills and test prep. They will assess your child, will meet with you to discuss his or her specific strengths and challenges, and will be able to focus specifically on your child's needs. Whereas Kumon was a good fit for the child who needed to drill math facts, these learning centers are perhaps more appropriate for the child who knows her math facts cold, but is having difficulty applying them.

That being said, Sylvan's cost places it out of the affordable range for many families. On the other hand, because they are franchised, each center does have some wiggle room on price. Believe it or not, you can discuss and negotiate the price before you sign a contract. If you have found a learning center branch that seems great and is within your budget, keep in mind that you will be asked to sign a contract that locks you in to a period of study that may extend 6 months or longer and will amount to a considerable expense. Before you sign, make sure that all your risk factors have been accounted for; for instance, since your child will be working closely with one particular tutor, the contract must allow for a trial period during which you can ascertain that the center is able to provide a tutor who has the necessary skills to work with your child. This means you get a chance to confirm that the tutor they hire has a thorough understanding of the material and of best methods for engaging your child's learning style.

Mathnasium

If your child's struggles are all math-related, Mathnasium is another option. This company is also a nationwide franchise, although the pay structure is somewhat different; overall, it may turn out to be less expensive than the other learning centers, especially if you use it several times a week, as it's a monthly fee for unlimited visits. Most branches' schedules are relatively flexible, so you may have an easier time arranging to bring your child when a tutor she works well with is there. Because it has assessments and child-specific plans of study but allows unlimited visits for a monthly fee, Mathnasium is popular with homeschool families.

Localized and Regional Centers

Here is a short list of learning centers that are more localized. All of these companies focus primarily on one-on-one test prep, but also provide academic tutoring and in some cases study skills. They are mostly geared toward older children.

- Academic Approach (Chicago, NYC, Boston)
- Advantage Testing (NYC and LA areas, plus a dozen other US locations)
- Appelrouth Tutoring (Atlanta, NYC, DC, Chicago, Seattle, LA)
- Chyten Education (10 locations in the northeastern US, and a few other US cities as well)
- Study Point (21 major US cities)

You may be able to find regional or local learning centers that offer one on one or group tutoring for free. These can be tricky to ferret out, but they do exist. For example, an organization called 826 has centers around the country that support students' creative and expository writing skills. Check the national website to see if there is an 826 center near you: 826national.org.

<u>Private Tutors</u>

One-on-one tutoring is a great solution in numerous situations. The pros of this choice include the fact that tutoring will truly be one-on-one, the work will be 100% adapted to your child's needs (and with an experienced, astute tutor, to his learning style as well), and perhaps most importantly, it eliminates the family dynamic. Because the rates for private tutors vary quite a bit, the cost could even be less than that of a learning center. Plus, it can happen at home, or at whatever location is most convenient for you, which is a boon to families with working parents or several children's schedules to juggle.

Take a close look at your child's struggles and see if you feel confident identifying what she needs from a tutor. Does she need help with a specific subject at school? Or help improving her study skills and organization? Does she just need someone to help her drill her math facts without the whole situation devolving into a fight?

Once you pinpoint your child's needs, you can start to look for a tutor. Here is a list of possible sources, to get you on the right path:

- Math facts can be drilled by a responsible neighborhood teenager;
- Local college campuses are good hunting grounds for affordable tutors in specific subjects, and some even sponsor official tutoring programs for free or at low cost;

- If you live near Caltech, UAA, Purdue, IUPUI, College of Charleston, or NYU Poly, try tutormatchingservice.com, where you can find certified college- and university-student tutors, many of whom volunteer their time for free;
- Some private and even some public schools will allow their teachers to tutor outside school hours (make sure to check school policy before trying this route);
- Many parents check Craigslist for a good private tutor (of course, if you go this route, you must do your own due diligence with regard to references);
- Many branches of the Salvation Army offer free tutoring and mentoring services;
- There are online sites that will help you find a tried and true tutor with good reviews from other parents. By far the largest database of tutors, with 75,000 tutors to choose from, is at Wyzant.com. A couple others are BuddySystem.com and the academic tutoring section of takelessons.com.

While planning, take the location into account. If schoolwork has been a source of contention in your family before now, then choosing to have the tutor work with your child at home while you're still at work or at a neutral location away from home could provide the fresh start your child needs. Consider your child's learning style; for some auditory learners, a coffeehouse with some well-modulated (instrumental!) music in the background might actually be a good spot to work; some kinesthetic learners will do well in the park, where they can move while they learn; other kids will be distracted by locations such as these and will need a nice quiet carrel upstairs in the local library. Selecting the work environment is an option available to you with a private tutor that you would not have at a learning center, so use it to your advantage.

Public-Private Workspace

Important protection for student and tutor alike: When finding that perfect workspace for your child and his new tutor, whom you don't know all that well, it must obviously provide the quiet the pair needs in order to focus. But it is also important that the space be visible and audible enough to ensure that there is no chance of harm coming to your child and to make even the question of any impropriety on the part of the tutor an impossibility. Your breakfast nook or your child's room with the door remaining open at all times are examples of such "public-private" workspaces.

"OK, I can handle all that, but which person should I hire?"

Keep in mind you're looking for the right tutor to fit not only your child's academic needs, but also his temperament and learning style. Read recommendations carefully, paying attention to comments about personality and teaching styles as well as academic gains. If there are no reviews or recommendations, don't be afraid to ask! A good tutor is eager to give you the phone number or email address of a happy parent who has offered to refer him. Don't be discouraged if the tutor your friend recommended or the first person you tried from Wyzant wasn't a good fit for your family. Soon enough you will find the right avenues to follow and the right questions to ask, and your child will have his very own miracle worker helping him understand the language everyone around him is speaking; soon he, too, will join in the conversation.

Online Tutoring

Yes! Not only can we order groceries, winter boots, and tubas, video chat with our friends in Hong Kong, track our finances, and order pizza online, we can get our kids tutored in cyberspace, too! Tutoring options online come in many shapes and sizes. Read carefully about what each service offers and seek outside confirmation that it's legit. There are many excellent services out there, but like with anything else on the net…well, you know how it is.

Scheduled Live Sessions with an Online Tutor

If your child is in elementary school or middle school, you are most likely looking for regularly scheduled sessions with the same tutor. There are many companies that provide this service live online. Your child will need a computer, a headset with a microphone, and a high-speed internet connection. When searching for a service of this type, make sure they are offering real time online sessions (not just check-ins with the tutor after the child completes work on her own). Here are just a few of the many companies out there:

- MindLaunch (mindlaunch.com)
    - Each student is matched with a teacher certified to teach in a US school system, rather than just certified by the company itself;
- Growing Stars (growingstars.com)
    - Most tutors have a master's degree in their fields;
- Sylvan Online Tutoring (sylvanlearning.com/tutoring/online-tutoring)
    - Uses the same approach as Sylvan Learning Centers, but offers one-on-one rather than group tutoring; requires a PC with Windows operating system)
- 1 to 1 Tutor (1to1Tutor.org)
    - Students can use an optional computer-attachable tablet to write on the 1 to 1 Tutor whiteboard. 1 to 1 Tutor also works with the Boys & Girls clubs of America to provide free tutoring service to eligible members; Contact your local branch of BGCA for information.

Instant Tutoring, 24/7

Some teenage students don't really need a regularly scheduled tutor, but do struggle from time to time with assignments you're not sure how to help them with. And knowing teenagers, crises like these often happen after midnight the night before an assignment is due. If this situation rings a bell with you, instant tutoring might be all your child needs to avoid poor grades on homework assignments or assignments not being turned in at all. Some of these services charge on a per-hour or per-minute basis, while others offer unlimited access for a monthly fee, so if your child has a difficult unit in trigonometry coming up, you can pay for one month of intense use and cancel when he moves into more manageable territory.

Just make sure the resource you choose is actually helping your child understand the material, not just selling him the answers at an hourly rate! You can do this by sitting side by side with your kid the first couple times he uses the service and watching how the interaction progresses. Yes, it'll mean a couple of nights' lost sleep, but afterward you'll (literally) rest assured knowing your credit card is paying for instruction rather than an easy cheat. There are literally dozens of instant tutoring sites online. Here are just a few to start your search:

- Eduboard.com allows the student to post her questions and then choose from different tutors and prices to get help;
- TutorVista.com provides unlimited tutoring for a surprisingly low monthly fee using tutors in India, most of whom have master's degrees;
- InstaEDU.com lets you search tutors for a particular topic and either choose one who is "ready to teach now" or schedule a session ahead of time.

…Which bring us to our next category:

The Hybrid

If your child needs the kind of spot-tutoring described above, but is a little more organized with her time, there are many online services that can be scheduled ahead of time, but still purchased on a pay-as-you-go basis. A few companies that focus on this type of service are:

- Tutapoint.com, which allows you to request a particular tutor you like;
- Smarthinking.com, which archives all sessions for students to review later;
- Moonlyt.com, which boasts "an army of supernerds".

These are just a few of the many hybrids out there.

"Isn't There an App for That?" – Totally Tech-Era Options

Is your child fascinated by all things digital? More and more, 100% digital-age tutoring options are popping up, and one of them could be the motivating factor that propels his learning. Until all schools are incorporating these options themselves (a small percentage do already), the programs may not connect exactly to your child's course of study, but they can be just what the principal ordered for certain situations.

There are basically two types of digital learning cropping up: Internet-Based Programs of Study and Tablet-Based learning. In these models, your child works independently online or on a tablet, using curricula designed specifically for digital learning, with periodic email contact or direct online guidance from a tutor.

One example of this is eTutor.com's guided study program, which uses a curriculum designed for internet learning; your child works independently using eTutor.com lesson modules and meets in real time online with a tutor once a week.

Some of these programs provide personalized programs, using point-of-learning analytics and a gamified learning experience. Two examples of this designed for K-8 students are TabTor Math, a tablet-based math skills program that allows the teacher to see the child's thinking process, and Dreambox Learning, a computer or tablet-based math program with lively graphics.

Even more motivating for kids than gamified learning is true game-based learning. This is gradually becoming easier to find, although as of yet, not in combination with true tutoring. For example, if you'd like to give your 8 to 12 year old child a boost in algebra before she even comes across it in the classroom, check out the Dragon Box app, which sneakily moves kids from a simple game to actual algebra equations before they even know what's happening.

Parent-Led Tutoring Using Online Resources

The most easily accessible and possibly the most affordable tutoring option is: you. Not every family can consider parent-led tutoring, as work schedules and family dynamics can sometimes be huge obstacles. But with a plethora of interesting, easy to use resources available online, parent-led tutoring is easier now than ever before.

There are many excellent, free or inexpensive resources that support tutoring in math, science, history, and social studies. English Language Arts is more difficult to support in this way, but there is material out there.

My two favorite online educational sites are both free aggregators of some of the best resources available. Both are non-profits, too, so it's an ad-free experience:

- A free account at powermylearning.com gives your K-12 student a gamified learning experience and access to a database of resources that is searchable by grade, subject and common core standards.

- At hippocampus.org you'll find videos, animations, and simulations on general education subjects for middle-school and high-school teachers and students.

Another good free general resource (although not ad-free) is internet4classrooms.com, which has links to free learning games for K-12 teachers–but it's free to parents and students as well.

And the general resource that is by far the most fun is Brainpop. It costs about $100 a year for access but is super-motivating for kids and hosts short animated films on hundreds of topics, as well as related quizzes and games. Even if you choose not to spring for an account, you can check out Brainpop's Free Stuff section for plenty of free material.

You would also have to pay about $100 a year to use mindsprinting.com. You get a lot for your money. Mindsprinting has progressive lessons in both math and English Language Arts.

For STEM subjects (the trendy term for "Science, Technology, Engineering and Math"), there's plenty of free and low-cost support out there. Here are just a few to get you started:

Science Sites:

> physicsclassroom.com
>
> schoolphysics.co.uk

Math Sites:

> KhanAcademy.com
>
> coolmath.com (age 13 and up)
>
> coolmath4kids.com (up to age 13)
>
> freemathelp.com
>
> Mathletics.com
>
> Intmath.com

Good sources for free printable worksheets:

> homeschoolmath.net
>
> beestar.org
>
> teacherspayteachers.com

<u>Special Situations</u>

For Gifted and Talented

If your super-smart kid is a little underserved at school, you're not alone. Teachers have a big job meeting the needs of kids performing below, at and above grade level. It's no surprise that the kids who are already performing above grade level often receive the least attention from busy, overworked teachers. If your child is feeling bored or even acting out at school because she's not being challenged in one or more areas of strength, the Johns Hopkins Center for Talented Youth (CTY) could be a good resource for you. CTY also makes a point of stating that it values diversity and provides special support for kids with academic, emotional, social, or behavioral differences. CTY offers numerous online courses for kids who qualify through testing. You can check out this program and the others CTY offers on their website: http://cty.jhu.edu

For Children with Dyslexia

If your child is dyslexic and you live in northeastern or north central US, there may be a free resource available to help. Children's Dyslexia Centers, Inc. offers free tutoring for kids with Dyslexia. Children are tutored once or twice a week after school and the program is tailored to each individual child. To find out if there is a branch near you, check the website: http://www.childrensdyslexiacenters.org/ContactUs.aspx

"My son failed Geometry! How can he graduate on time?"

Credit Recovery

Your high school student may be facing an even more serious situation than just lagging grades; in high school, a failed course can mean a student lacks the credits he needs to graduate on time, or the courses required to enter a particular higher education program. If your child is facing a situation such as this one, you will not only want to help him grasp concepts and master skills, but also to attain the credits needed to graduate on time and, if he is headed for college, to enter the field of study that interests him. Your child's guidance counselor is of course the first person to turn to if this situation arises. Many public school systems now have more options for credit recovery than summer school or repeating a grade.

If you find that your school district has little to offer, or that your child has a specific need or time frame the school system can't address, you can also find numerous programs online that will provide the courses and credits your child needs. In other words, in addition to continuing to attend his high school classes, he can "enroll" in one of these to make up the credit he needs to graduate. I am listing just a few below to get you started, but a simple internet search of the phrase "high school credit recovery" will give you dozens of options.

- Apex Learning (www.apexlearning.com)
- Compass Learning (www.compasslearning.com)
- K12 (www.k12.com/who-we-help/credit-recovery)
- The Keystone School (http://keystoneschoolonline.com/credit-recovery)

The key to choosing the right online credit recovery program is twofold. First, just like with all the other tutoring options we've explored, it's crucial to find the solution that works best for your child—especially if he's already been struggling with this particular subject matter. Second – and no less important! – is confirming that your child's school (or the one to which he is applying) will accept credit from the institution you've chosen. Be sure to contact the school and verify that the program you've selected has all the necessary accreditations to be recognized on your child's transcript.

Keeping the End Goal in Mind

How long will my child need an off-site learning center or some form of tutoring? That's a question that may go unanswered for a while. It will depend on the quality of the resource, the level of your child's efforts, and your goals. Just to give you some context, though, studies show that you can have an impact with targeted instruction at a minimum of 36 hours. When a child begins an SES intervention that uses targeted items, he is expected to improve in 30-40 hours of instruction; likewise, tutoring giant Sylvan Learning seems to agree with that statistic, as they guarantee one grade level's growth in 36 hours.

Once you enter the outside-of-school tutoring world, it can be hard to know when it's time to leave. Set a goal, so your child won't be frustrated. The goal can be passing a course, reaching grade level in a particular subject, bringing up report card grades, or hitting a target on standardized tests and offer small rewards for milestones reached along the way. Your child's hard work is worth celebrating!

A special trip to her favorite ice cream store just with mom or dad for having reached an attainable mini-goal might be all the acknowledgment and incentive she needs to keep forging forward with something that has been a real challenge for her. Unless you've determined that your child will need ongoing support in one or more areas (and that's a real possibility, too), you should plan your exit strategy now. In either case, it's a great idea consider sitting down with your child, developing some goals together, and building in a few rewards as incentive.

CHAPTER TWELVE

504: A CIVIL RIGHTS ISSUE!

When you think about "civil rights," the phrase probably conjures up images of marches on Washington in the 1960s…or voting rights…or freedom of speech…or marriage equality. You probably don't think of…your child's classroom. After all, schools were desegregated several decades ago, right?

I'm not going to touch that question. But I will say that your child's right to a ***Free and Appropriate Public Education (FAPE)*** absolutely *is* a civil rights issue. And there is a federal civil rights law that says so.

The relevant part of Section 504 of the Rehabilitation Act of 1973 states:

"No otherwise qualified individual with a disability in the United States, as defined in section 705(20) of this title, shall, solely by reason of her or his disability, be excluded from the participation in, be denied the benefits of, or be subjected to discrimination under any program or activity receiving Federal financial assistance…"

A Legal Term, Not a Label

I feel that this box is important enough that it bears repeating in both Chapters 11 and 12:

Please do not be put off by my use of the word "disability" here and in the following chapter. I do so because it is the legal language that allows your child to get help. What your child is being evaluated for is the presence and nature of a "disability"–as defined by IDEA–that affects his or her learning.

Take a deep breath. The D word carries some heavy baggage with it, and I am going to ask you to try to leave as much as possible of that baggage behind. Yes, your child may have a 'disability'. Breathe! This DOES NOT mean that your child cannot or will not excel in school, or in life. The reality is that WE ALL have disabilities–you do, your child's teacher does, his evaluators do, whether they fall under that moniker according to IDEA or not. If your child needed glasses, would you hesitate to state what was wrong and seek help? Of course not! This is no different. When you see the word 'disability' in this text, read 'difference.'

As soon as a law is passed, of course, memoranda are issued and regulations are drafted (and lawsuits are brought) to clarify all the verbiage contained therein. Section 504 was no different:

For a student to be an "otherwise qualified individual," he must be roughly between the ages of three and twenty-two.

A person "...with a disability" has been defined by federal law as "...any person who: (i) has a mental or physical impairment that substantially limits one or more major life activity; (ii) has a record of such an impairment; or (iii) is regarded as having such an impairment"

I could now define "a physical or mental impairment," and "substantially," and "a major life activity," but life's too short, and I can tell you just want me to get to the point. I will say, though, that there is no comprehensive list of the disabilities, disorders and illnesses that could be considered "physical or mental impairment[s]" for the purposes of Section 504, because the drafters of the law didn't want anyone who might need the law's protection to be excluded and denied help.

That said, here are some examples of specific disabilities often requiring accommodations:

- Cerebral Palsy;
- Tourette's;
- Bipolar Disorder;
- Allergies;
- Chemical Sensitivities;
- Learning Disabilities, such as (but not limited to) Dyslexia;
- ADD/ADHD;
- Anorexia/Bulimia;
- Obesity and related issues;
- Poor vision or visual processing challenges;
- Poor hearing or auditory processing challenges;
- Epilepsy;
- Paralysis;
- Diabetes;
- Cystic Fibrosis;
- Other extended illnesses, such as cancer or heart disease.

So here's the bottom line, where students are concerned:

Section 504 of the Rehabilitation Act ensures that no one with a disability can be excluded from participating in federally funded activities, which include public schooling. Section 504 affords students the accommodations they need to be able to compete with their classmates.

These accommodations can take many different forms. Here are some of the many accommodations that can be made for students with physical or mental disabilities:

- Giving extra time on tests for a student who has slower processing abilities;
- Allowing the use of a computer for all note-taking and test-taking for a student with a disability that impedes her ability to write at the same speed as her classmates (or, perhaps, to write at all);
- Permitting the use of an elevator for a student who is wheelchair bound or who has difficulty walking the stairs;
- Giving two sets of textbooks, one for use at school and one for use at home to a student who has difficulty organizing (and thus forgets his textbooks most days) or who has a physical challenge that makes carrying them back and forth between school and home difficult;
- Providing an aide to read test questions aloud to a student who either has a visual disability or who has difficultly retaining attention and focus;
- Providing a health para-professional for a child with an ongoing illness or physical disability;
- Receiving medication during the school day;
- Removing allergens or chemicals from the environment;
- Allowing the use of a recording device in the classroom;
- Allowing greater access to a school social worker for a child with anxiety;
- Adapting physical education class as per her physician's recommendation for an obese child;
- Providing a private place and carving out time for a child recovering from cancer to rest quietly, and arranging for home tutoring during treatments.

Basically, there are no restrictions on what qualifies as an accommodation, if something actually does the job of removing barriers to learning in the regular general ed classroom for a particular child. If you are requesting a reasonable accommodation on a "504", you should never take "Oh, no, Section 504 doesn't permit *that…*" for an answer!

> **Section 504 of the Rehabilitation Act ensures that no one with a disability can be excluded from participating in federally funded activities, which include public schooling.**
> **Section 504 affords students the accommodations they need to be able to compete with their classmates.**

I think you're getting the point. Section 504 applies to children for whom specific accommodations or modifications are sufficient to support them in school. In other words, a 504 is appropriate for a child who does not need the additional special education supports or services that would be provided by an IEP (which I will discuss in the next chapter). But they do need accommodations or modifications so that they can compete within general education classrooms. Accommodations such as those listed above enable children with issues such as those listed above to participate in classroom activities to the same extent as children without disabilities *because such accommodations eliminate the barriers to their learning in that setting.* (How hard the children then work and how they ultimately perform is then up to them. Accommodations are not a guarantee of success; they are just a playing-field leveler that gives children with disabilities an equal opportunity to succeed.)

It would be nice if these accommodations magically appeared for each disabled student, according to her need. But, obviously, they don't – they need to be secured. So how does this happen? Or, to put it more actively, how can you secure such accommodations for your child who needs them?

> **If you are requesting a reasonable accommodation on a "504",**
> **you should never take "Oh, no, Section 504 doesn't permit that…" for an answer!**

Securing Accommodations Under Section 504 (a.k.a., informally, "Getting a 504"):

Who can refer a child for evaluation?

Short answer: Anyone. A parent, a doctor, a child's teacher(s) or the administrators of the child's school, anyone. In theory, a school should be flagging cases and referring them for evaluation, but in practice, it is invariably the parent who must get the ball rolling. But here's the catch: the Office for Civil Rights (OCR) has determined that "the school district must also have reason to believe that the child is in need of services under Section 504 due to a disability." So you, the parent, can ask for an evaluation of your child, but you cannot demand one.

What if the school district won't evaluate my child?

There is a chance that the district may determine that your child is not qualified, i.e., that the child does not have a physical or mental impairment that substantially limits a major life activity warranting accommodations. If this happens, however, the school district must furnish you with written notice of your procedural rights (i.e., how to appeal the decision) under Section 504. REMEMBER: This is a civil rights issue! If you believe your child warrants the protection provided by Section 504, you have a due process right to appeal the school district's denial!

But let's dwell on the positive. Let's assume that if you've ascertained a good reason to seek Section 504 accommodations for your child, your child's teachers and you are in complete agreement, and your child is referred for evaluation:

Who does the evaluation?

A committee from the school district is convened to evaluate your child. A parent can request to be on the committee but does not have an automatic right to be there; the decision to include or not include the parent is up to the district. I'm happy to tell you, though, that a great many districts do include the parent as a matter of course. At least one person directly familiar with your child's disabilities should be on the committee, as well as a person with expertise in the sorts of accommodations that can assist your child with the type(s) of challenge(s) she's facing.

What information is used to determine eligibility?

Your child does not need to undergo special additional testing to receive accommodations under Section 504. The Section 504 Team reviews all available information, including:

- Past and recent test scores and other assessments done in class;
- Any other evaluations;
- Teachers' comments and input;
- Parents' comments and input; and
- Reports and recommendations from health professionals and/or mental health professionals.

How often is a child reevaluated?

Section 504 does not specify how often a child should be reassessed. As part of the Section 504 plan for your child, the committee should determine when the next reassessment should take place. Most districts reassess Section 504 plans on a yearly basis.

Then what happens?

The committee must provide you, the parent, with written notice of the results of the meeting, as well as written guidelines for appealing anything in the Plan you disagree with. The school must comply with the Section 504 Plan and must designate an employee who is charged with carrying out the Plan.

> **In theory, a school should be flagging cases and referring them for evaluation, but in practice, it is invariably the parent who must get the ball rolling.**

My child's teacher is already bending the rules for my child. Why go through all of this?

You might think you do not need a formal plan under Section 504 because your school is informally already giving your child the exact accommodations he needs without going through the rigmarole, but I'm here today to tell you – go through the rigmarole! Here's why:

First of all, you will not be offending anyone at your child's school by seeking to put in writing what is already in place. So don't worry about that. Worry, instead, about what might happen if your child's teacher or school administrator has a family emergency or some other reason why he suddenly needs to leave, and the new teacher or administrator doesn't "get it," and simply doesn't want to be bothered to continue to implement the accommodations. A Section 504 plan is a legal document – it legally obligates the school district to follow through on every provision it contains to protect and aid your child.

With the protection of a 504, you need never worry that a misguided, ignorant, or simply lazy adult will harm your child, as happened with the child of a close friend of mine. Her son, a sweet and talented boy who suffers from debilitating anxiety, was set back profoundly in his progress by an arrogant administrator who chose to substitute his own judgment for that of the mental health professionals. The administrator refused to recognize the terrible pain the child experiences during fire drills due to acute sound and light sensitivity. He also downplayed the oppressive anxiety that affected every moment of the child's school day, since the boy never knew when yet another painful drill might suddenly assault his senses. That would never have happened had a Section 504 Plan been in place. The administrator would have been required by law to remove the child from the premises before each drill took place, and if he failed to do so, my friend would have had recourse under the law to force him to comply.

Even though this example is an extreme case of mismanagement and we know that most educators are caring and thoughtful in their decisions that affect the children they oversee, children must always be protected from the possibility of neglect or abuse. Section 504 was created to assure that a child's access to accommodations or modifications would not be dependent on a teacher or administrator's opinions or whims. Therefore, it is never appropriate for a school to simply put accommodations in place informally. If a child needs the accommodations to be able to compete in school, the school should be referring the child for a Section 504 Plan. And if the school hasn't done so of its own accord, you should request that they do. They're not doing your child a favor – it's your child's civil right.

PROTECTION AGAINST BULLYING!

Section 504 not only protects your child's right to compete in the classroom, it also protects your child's right not to be discriminated against for her disability...and this includes BULLYING. If your child is being harassed (or worse!) for her disability, notify your school immediately. The school must take prompt steps to end the discrimination. Period. And if they don't act quickly and decisively enough, go over their heads to the district, and also look for a child advocacy organization in your area that can step in on your child's behalf. Right. Now.

CHAPTER THIRTEEN

INTRODUCING THE INDIVIDUALIZED EDUCATION PLAN (IEP)

In the previous chapters, you and I have talked about the various kinds of support your child automatically receives at school through RTI, the types of support you can provide outside school and at home, and how to get accommodations through Section 504 of the Rehabilitation Act that your child might need in the classroom and/or during standardized testing in order to be playing on a level field with his classmates.

But what if all that isn't enough?

This chapter is really for a very small number of school-aged children…but if you're reading it because you fear that the assists I've discussed prior to now are not adequate to help your child, please do read on. Your child does not score "brownie points" for toughing it out in those early years when additional support can do the most for him. Only a small percentage of my readership's children will need this chapter, but if your child is one of them, I'm glad you're here.

Marissa, a kindergartner whose mom kept her home during the preschool years, was struggling in class. She loved her teacher and her classmates, but was unable to sit in her chair and focus during work time and had a hard time keeping up with lessons on the rug. At first, Marissa's teacher suspected that her struggles were simply a result of the early education she had missed by skipping formal preschool, so she followed RTI protocol and pulled her out for special small group work and also asked her mother to bring her in for the school's morning program 3 days a week. But after two months in RTI, with close monitoring by the grade-level team, Marissa was even further behind, and it didn't seem that accommodations under Section 504 would catch her up. And so, Marissa's teacher suggested that she be assessed by the school's staff. By the end of the year, Marissa had been assessed, the school psychologist had discovered that Marissa was dyslexic and dyspraxic (which means she had trouble getting her body to do what her brain wanted it to do), the Individualized Education Program (IEP) team had met and crafted an IEP plan, and Marissa had begun sessions with the Speech and Language Pathologist, the Occupational Therapist, and the reading specialist during school hours. By the middle of first grade, it became clear that Marissa needed an "inclusion" classroom (which I'll describe later in this chapter), and her IEP was revised to reflect this change of placement. Marissa thrived there and was reintroduced to a mainstream classroom in fourth grade, where she continued to thrive with ongoing speech and occupational therapies.

If you are a parent reading this chapter right now, most likely either

- your K-12 student is struggling, and you haven't yet come to something in this book that resonated with you as an option that might really help,
- you have been notified that a teacher or staff member of your child's school has made a referral for evaluation;
- your child has been receiving some form of early childhood services and already has an IEP, but is soon to transition into kindergarten; or
- your child has an IEP and has transitioned to elementary school or beyond, and you are looking for support in the sometimes murky, always challenging IEP world.

If you're in one of the first two groups, read on, as you have most likely now found what you need. If you're in the third, I suggest skimming through until you get to **Transitioning from Early Intervention to Kindergarten**, and pick up reading there, and if you're in the fourth, you may wish to skip down to **Subsequent IEP Meetings**.

OK. Here comes help!

If your child is struggling, and none of the things we've discussed so far offer enough support, then it is likely that he needs to be assessed by a team of professionals in several ways in order to discover what is holding him back. Don't worry! There is a process for that. And once the difficulties have been ferreted out, your child needs a plan in place (called an "IEP," which stands for "Individualized Education Plan," a.k.a., "Individualized Education Program") that will affirm his right to the support he needs and legally guarantee that he gets it. There's a process for that, too. Don't get me wrong, the system is by no means infallible, but I am going to walk you through what is available to you and how to navigate the system so that you have the best chance of setting up exactly the supports your child needs for success in school.

You have a right to translation!

Don't let language be a barrier to getting all the help and information you need. Both the NCLB and IDEA laws I discussed in Chapter Two include requirements that your child's school communicate important information, such as special education information, in your native language. You have a right to receive written results of assessments and evaluations in your native language, or, if this is not possible, to have the results translated for you orally. Your child has the right to be evaluated for special education services in his native language. And you have the right to an interpreter in the room with you during all teacher conferences and IEP meetings.

"What exactly is an IEP?"

An IEP, or Individualized Education Plan, is a detailed plan designed for the specific needs of the child, outlining goals for his academic progress and listing the supports necessary to help him achieve those goals. It is also a legal document that, once signed, must be implemented by the school system.

I will explain what is in the document in greater detail below, but for now, let's sort out how to get one in place to help your child:

Step One: Requesting Referral for Evaluation

Under the IDEA (which we discussed in Chapter Two), you have the right to ask for an assessment to determine what issues are at the root of your child's struggles in school. The assessment is done for two reasons: first, in order to show that your child is legally 'eligible' for services, since there is a list of those disabilities that qualify a child for an IEP; second, to discover exactly what's going on and have solid data from which to work when developing the plan to support him.

Don't worry about the 'eligibility' part at the moment. If you're reading this now, and have not decided to skip the chapter, it's a pretty dependable likelihood that your child is eligible. A host of issues–running the gamut from hearing, vision or speech impairment, to physical difference of ability, to learning differences, to autism spectrum challenges–are included in the list of disabilities that render children eligible for IEPs. In most cases, if

- your child has a challenge that most of his peers do not face, and
- his schoolwork is affected by it, and
- the issues he's struggling with cannot be addressed with accommodations or modifications through a 504,

...he's eligible!

So, knowing that, here's how you get started. Every IEP begins with a 'referral for evaluation'. That just means you have formally requested that a school official refer your child for evaluation. You can do this by making the request *in writing* to the school principal, psychologist or social worker. If you're not comfortable doing it yourself, ask the school social worker for help. When you get a home, start a file that you will keep along with all your other important papers, and file a copy of your request as the first document you save.

Timeliness: It's the Law

If your child needs an IEP, she needs it ASAP. And the law ensures that she will get it, stat.

- Once your child has been referred for evaluation, the evaluation process must be completed within 60 calendar days within the school year (summer vacation is excluded). The clock starts ticking when you sign the "Consent to Evaluate" form.
- Once the evaluation process is complete, the IEP meeting must take place within 30 calendar days.
- Once the meeting has occurred and an IEP is issued, the plan must be enacted within 10 school days.
- Once your child has an IEP in place, the IEP must be reviewed annually at a meeting. (Of course, you have a right to request additional meetings at any time; you need not wait a full year should the IEP need revising.)
- Once every three years at the most, your child must be reevaluated. (Of course, if you believe that your child needs testing in a particular area sooner than that, you can make that formal request with the school.)

Keep a Paper Trail

Keep copies of all documents relating to your child's IEP, and start a notebook as well. All of your actions with regard to special education for your child— as well as the school's and local DOE's actions—are governed by law. Therefore, it's important to document everything, including taking detailed notes about what you said and what was said to you on particular dates during meetings or on the phone.

A parent is not the only person who can make a request for initial referral. The law also allows teachers and professional staff involved with your child's education to request evaluation, as well as his physician or a judge overseeing a family court matter. Don't be shocked! That's a good thing; it means that many children whose parents are not aware that their children are struggling are given support because concerned adults in the community noticed that they needed help. So if you are reading this because you received written notice that someone filed a request for evaluation of your child, don't worry. There is no implication that you have done anything wrong or are in any way responsible for your child's difficulties in school. Every individual has challenges, and some of these challenges require extra or different attention in an academic setting. And you were not remiss in not knowing this – you are probably not a professional educator and are certainly not in the classroom with your child every day. It is common for referrals to come from the education professionals who work with our children. And, regardless of who initiates the process, many of the issues that parents and children used to be left to deal with as best they could without support are now better understood and can be improved with the right interventions.

Eligibility Exceptions That Prove the Rule

As I said, if your child has a challenge that affects his ability to learn in a general ed classroom, even with accommodations, he may be eligible for an IEP…but there are a few exceptions to this rule. Kids whose central challenge is Sensory Integration Disorder, OCD, ADD, or ADHD are sometimes found ineligible. In most cases, however, eligibility can be established in another way. A child with these challenges can almost always be given a related diagnosis that places him in an IDEA category. Children with ADHD, for example, are often placed in a speech and language category. If you feel sure that 504 accommodations or modifications will not be sufficient for your child, and that he needs services or counseling in addition, meet with your child's pediatrician or other health professional before the IEP meeting to discuss possible categories under which he might be eligible.

Charlie's parents were very concerned. His "turning 5" meeting was coming up—the meeting that would decide the details of his transition from early childhood intervention to school age services. Charlie had difficulty sitting still in Pre-K, leaned on other children in line, and fell down and hurt himself often. He cried when the other kids made too much noise at lunch. Sensory Processing Disorder made it difficult for Charlie to feel comfortable in his school environment and to behave appropriately during class, so Charlie had been receiving OT to help him regulate his sensory system. Charlie's parents knew SPD was not considered an acceptable category to get services through his IEP once he was in kindergarten, so they sat down with his OT and scoured his records and tests to figure out a work-around. The OT had been working with Charlie on fine motor skills and strengthening his core, as he was late starting to write his letters and often flopped or 'W-sat'. Although Charlie's hypotonia or 'low tone' was a minor issue in comparison to SPD, it was a medical diagnosis that would fall indisputably under "other impairment." Charlie's parents asked his pediatrician for a letter stating this diagnosis and took it with them to his "turning 5." It was a good thing they did, because the first thing the district rep said when they sat at the table was, "I don't see how this child is eligible."

A Legal Term, Not a Label

I feel that this box is important enough that it bears repeating in both Chapters 11 and 12:

Please do not be put off by my use of the word "disability" here and in the preceding chapter. I do so because it is the legal language that allows your child to get help. What your child is being evaluated for is the presence and nature of a "disability"—as defined by IDEA—that affects his or her learning.

Take a deep breath. The D word carries some heavy baggage with it, and I am going to ask you to try to leave as much as possible of that baggage behind. Yes, your child may have a 'disability'. Breathe! This DOES NOT mean that your child cannot or will not excel in school, or in life. The reality is that WE ALL have disabilities—you do, your child's teacher does, his evaluators do, whether they fall under that moniker according to IDEA or not. If your child needed glasses, would you hesitate to state what was wrong and seek help? Of course not! This is no different. When you see the word 'disability' in this text, read 'difference.'

Step Two: Evaluation

Before evaluation takes place, your child's school will develop and must share with you a written evaluation plan. The plan will list all the tests and observations they plan to conduct. Most often, the school will use its own staff to conduct testing, but if they do not have the necessary resources on staff, they can use outside resources that are approved by their DOE to conduct testing. Read the plan carefully and ask questions! Make sure you understand the purpose of each test. If there is a challenge your child faces that doesn't seem to be addressed by the types of tests on the plan, describe your concerns to the IEP coordinator, team leader, or school psychologist and ask what kinds of tests relate to your child's difficulties, so they can be added.

The initial evaluation to determine if your child has a disability will include:

- A comprehensive psycho-educational evaluation that looks at what your child knows and how he or she learns;
- A social history of your child's developmental and family history, often from your pregnancy or your child's birth to present;
- An observation of your child in the classroom;
- Other tests that may be appropriate for your child, such as speech, language or functional behavior assessments as needed;
- Assessments that include a review of school records, teacher assessments, and parent and student interviews;
- In some cases, a report of a recent physical examination of your child. If a physical exam is required and you have trouble obtaining one, the school will arrange one at no cost to you.

These evaluations will assess your child's skills and abilities and identify the areas of need that affect his or her school performance, and they will inform the design of the plan to help him succeed.

You can also choose to have your child tested privately, and if you share those results, the IEP Team must consider the results of that testing when devising your child's IEP. But private testing is very expensive, and will remove your child from even more class time, so I suggest asking around among parents in your community to discover their level of satisfaction with the testing provided in your school or district. If you do have your child tested privately, you are not required to share the test results with the school if you don't wish to.

If your child is tested by the school, and you are not satisfied with the quality or results of the testing, you can contact the school (again, do it *in writing* and keep a copy in your file). State that you do not agree with the test results and are requesting an IEE (Independent Educational Evaluation–and no, educators never run out of initialisms!). The school must then pay for an IEE or start a due process hearing at which it will have to prove that its evaluation was appropriate for your child. If the school does pay for an IEE, however, there will be limits, such as a cap to the cost, or a list of approved providers you can choose from. Whether the school foots the bill or not, you retain the right to have your child tested privately and to have those results considered alongside the school's results.

Step Three: Scheduling a Meeting (The District Does This)

Now that you are armed with a pile of information about your child's strengths and challenges, you have a much better picture of what's going on, and so do the teachers and staff at his school. The next step in this process is the IEP Meeting. This is a meeting of everyone on your child's IEP Team.

> **"What exactly is an IEP?"**
>
> **An IEP, or Individualized Education Plan (also called
> an Individualized Education Program),
> is a detailed plan designed for the specific needs of the child,
> outlining goals for his academic progress and
> listing the supports necessary to help him achieve those goals.
> It is also a legal document that, once signed, must be implemented by the school system.**

The school must notify you in advance of the scheduled date and time for the meeting, and must make every effort to schedule the meeting so that you can participate. That being said, if you receive notice of the meeting and do not respond, and then do not show up for the meeting, it will take place without you. Don't be offended by this; this provision in the laws is intended to protect children whose parents don't advocate for them, allowing concerned teachers to move forward with a process they think will help the children they are teaching.

Step Four: The IEP Meeting

This is a meeting of all the people who have been assembled to help your child succeed academically. In most cases, everyone in the room will genuinely care about your child's welfare and will be working toward his success. That being said, at every IEP meeting, there is a chance that one or more members are under pressure to cut costs (read: be stingy with expensive services your child might benefit from). And at every IEP meeting, there are likely to be several earnest but differing opinions as to what will best serve your child. If possible, discuss the results of the testing ahead of time with those you trust, and think through what interventions you think would best serve your child. Enter the meeting with a balance of openness, knowing that professionals in the room might have helpful ideas and good plans, but also with resolve, as you know your child best, and you have the most at stake in securing the help he needs.

> ### Putting Your Head in the Sand Just Gives You a Sandy Head
>
> Never ignore communications from your child's school, thinking that an issue will go away if you ignore it! As a parent, the law is very much on your side, providing many rights to protect and support your child. But if you ignore official communications and skip IEP meetings, those present at the meetings can and most likely will make legally binding decisions that affect your child, without your input. This can even extend to your child's placement in a particular kind of class or school.

Does it sound a little daunting? Ok, then let's make it clear what will happen during this process and put your mind at ease, because at every step there are safeguards you can make use of. First of all, who's on the team?

The IEP Team consists of:

- YOU! (Wait, to clarify: You, empowered!);
- At least one of your child's general education teachers;
- A school district representative (this may be a separate district rep, or the district may be represented by a school staff member);
- A person qualified to interpret the test results, such as a special education teacher or a school psychologist;
- If he is 16 years or older, your child.

You also have the right to have any of these people present at the meeting:

- If needed, a translator;
- A professional or volunteer parent advocate;
- A friend;
- A person who has worked with your child, such as a caregiver or outside teacher who has relevant observations of your child's needs and abilities;
- A professional of your choosing, such as a doctor or therapist, who can shed light on your child's educational struggles

If there is someone whose input you'd like at the meeting, but he or she can't be there, that's ok. You are allowed to have an advocate, spouse, health professional or other support attend the meeting by phone or video conference. You can also submit a written statement from any of these people to support the ideas you'd like to present.

Creation of the IEP

The IEP meeting has been convened so that the team can create your child's IEP, the legal document that will detail the supports your child will receive in school and the type of placement deemed appropriate for her. But in almost every case, a team member from your child's school will arrive at the meeting with a draft of the IEP form already filled out. Contact your child's school before the meeting to find out if this will be the case, and if so, ask to be sent a copy of the draft in advance. Carefully consider what the team member proposes; often the draft IEP has been drawn up by a therapist or psychologist who administered one or more of your child's tests, and who has experience with children presenting similar challenges.

Here's what will be in the document:

- A statement of your child's present levels of performance, based on all the tests and information in the evaluation;
- Specific goals for the coming year;
- Specific supports, services, accommodations, and/or modifications recommended for your child; this may include school-based services in a general education context, placement in a special inclusion program, or placement in a solely special ed program.

Keep in mind that you are not at the IEP meeting merely to sign off on whatever is proposed. This group of people is called an IEP TEAM for a reason: you are mandated––by law––to work as a team to develop the IEP. There should be healthy discussion around the table as to the pros and cons of what is proposed in the draft.

If all goes well, you and the other team members will be able to edit the draft until everyone is satisfied that it will meet your child's needs. The school will then draw up a clean, revised document and send you a copy, after which you have ten days to object if there is still something incorrect in the document. Make sure you are happy with the IEP, because as I said before, it is *legally binding*; this means that even if they agree with you about your objections, the school is required by law to do whatever is mandated in the document until another meeting is held and changes to the IEP are made.

Of course, there is always the chance that you cannot come to an agreement with the other members of the team. If this happens, don't panic. Simply explain politely that you don't agree and can't sign the document. In some cases, when the others in the room realize you are not going to back down, they will offer a compromise or agree to your wishes and amend the document. In others, you will have to go to mediation or a hearing in order to resolve your differences. We'll talk about that below.

Your Child's Placement

Before you started this process, you might not have given much thought to the type of classroom your child would learn in. A classroom is a classroom, right? Actually, no. There are many types of classrooms, and one of the jobs of the IEP team is to assure that your child has the right 'placement'. In other words, your child has been placed in the kind of classroom that is best for his or her learning needs.

Here are typical types of placement available in most school districts:

- *General Education Classroom*

Your child will be fully integrated into a regular general education classroom, and will receive the supports mandated in the IEP either in the classroom (the resource/IEP teacher or therapist will 'push-in' to the classroom), or in the Resource Room or Related Services Rooms (your child will be pulled out of the classroom for services).

- *Inclusion Classroom, also known as ICT (Integrated Co-Teaching) or CTT (Collaborative Team Teaching) Classrooms*

Your child will be integrated with other general education students as well as other students with special needs; within the classroom, there will be no distinction or labeling of kids as gen-ed or special-ed, but your child will receive the support mandated in the IEP either through push-in or pull-out services, as above. The class is taught by a team consisting of one general ed teacher and one special ed teacher. All the kids in the class benefit from the improved teacher/student ratio.

- *Self-Contained Special Education Classroom*

Your child will spend the day in a special ed classroom, with a much smaller class size and special education teacher.

- *Out of District Placement*

Your child will be placed in a program outside of the general education environment, in order to meet his or her needs.

> **In theory, the IEP is designed around the child's needs,**
> **and the placement is chosen to fit the IEP.**
> **Don't be railroaded into signing an IEP that is designed**
> **to force the child to fit the placement.**

Change of placement and change of location are not equivalent. Your child can be moved into a new placement at the same school she's in now (from general education into ICT, for instance, or from a self-contained special ed into a mainstreamed classroom with "pull-outs" for services). Your child can also be moved to a different school, but if the type of placement is not changed, services will remain the same without a change to the IEP. If you're attending an IEP meeting in the middle of a school year, be aware that the right kind of placement for your child may not exist in her current school, and that team members may be recommending that your child be given the right placement at a different location; likewise, be aware that staff may be reluctant to admit they do not have the right placement, and may have had clouded judgment when recommending placement within the same location.

Eighth grader Natalie had been at the same small APS (Approved Private School, a school the Department of Ed funds to educate children with particular special needs) since pre-K. This year, at her IEP meeting, the Team Leader suggested continuing the same services Natalie had the year before. Natalie's mom was surprised—she felt Natalie had made significant gains in the last two years, and wondered why services should remain the same. Although the mandated three years had not passed since Natalie's last evaluation, Natalie's mother requested that the school conduct a new evaluation and re-convene the

IEP Team meeting afterward. When the Team met again, Natalie's mom had the results in hand. She and her husband had met with their favorite staff member at the school, Natalie's OT, and the three of them decided Natalie was ready for a new placement—at a mainstream school. They convinced the other team members, and once the IEP was signed, Natalie and her parents started researching schools in their area. Natalie felt like she had become a big fish in a small pond at her old school, and she wanted the excitement of a big high school. When they toured a large, sunny high school that was not in their district, Natalie fell in love. Placement at that school was not one of their official options, but Natalie was insistent, so Natalie's mom secured a meeting with the principal. One of the skills Nat had learned at her old school was self-advocacy; Natalie herself explained how she felt about the school, and made the request for a special waiver that would allow her to attend it. She even outlined the services the school would need to provide to meet her needs, which included speech therapy and OT. The principal was so impressed with the young woman that he granted the waiver. The following fall, Natalie became a smiling, mainstreamed ninth-grader.

"Best Possible Placement"

The truth is, it is rare to get *exactly* the right placement for any child. And that's true whether your child has special needs or not. Every child would benefit from small class size, as shown in multiple studies, but most American children are learning in classrooms that are crowded to the max; likewise, many children who require special education but excel in academics end up having to compromise either the supports that would help them or the advanced learning environment that best suits them. Depending on your child's needs, seats in a classroom that is *perfect* for her may be very limited or may not exist at all where you live, even if you're able to pay top dollar for a private school. Ultimately you will have to weigh the pros and cons of different placements and make compromises. That being said, among the choices available to you, there does exist a 'best possible placement' for your child. The other members of the IEP team may not always agree with you what that placement is, so you may have to fight for what your child needs. More about that further on in the chapter.

Transitioning to Kindergarten (a.k.a., "The Turning Five Meeting")

If your child already has an IEP as you read this, you already know a lot about how it works. But when your child transitions to kindergarten, a major change takes place, for which you need to be prepared. Even if your child's needs have not changed one iota, the jurisdiction under which your child falls and the factors that allow him to receive services and accommodations do.

In early childhood, federal laws require that children be given supports if they show developmental delays, or the likelihood of developmental delays, no matter how those delays affect her ability to function in any particular environment. Once your child enters kindergarten, however, that is no longer the case. Federal laws only require school districts to give accommodations and support to children who have one or more of specific list of disabilities, and then only if their academic achievement (*not* their social, physical, or emotional well-being) is adversely affected by those disabilities.

The Transition IEP Meeting

If your child already has an IEP prior to kindergarten, the jurisdiction will now shift to your school district, and the person or team that has been in charge of your child's IEP up until this point will transfer her records to an office or school in your district. You will be notified of the "Transition IEP Meeting," also known as the "Turning Five Meeting," with the team that will decide your child's placement and services when she enters kindergarten. If the meeting takes place in a school, it may or may not be the school your child will eventually attend.

As with any IEP meeting, do not ignore this notice. Even if you think the services your child has received up until now have been sufficient, and she will not need support in kindergarten, or if you think everything is going well and should just remain the same, you cannot assume either of these outcomes will happen if you are not at the meeting. If you want services to continue, and if you have an opinion regarding what those services should include, it is most important that you be there! If the team does not officially choose to end the IEP, services must continue, and placement will be made accordingly; you may need to fight to ensure this. And services that were a given in early childhood may be ones you have to fight for tooth and nail for a school-age child; they will not automatically be continued in kindergarten.

Preparing for the Transition Meeting

- Hopefully you have kept good files documenting your child's needs. Gather and make copies of all this information. Also seek statements from your child's teacher and/or service providers that support her need for services.
- If you feel it would be helpful, arrange to have a caregiver, teacher, or service provider at the meeting, either in person or by phone or video conference.
- Talk to your child's pediatrician, and if there is a medical diagnosis that supports you child's need for services, request a letter to that effect, particularly if you are concerned with eligibility.
- Before the meeting, talk to your child's teachers and service providers and try to develop an idea of the right placement for your child.
- Visit as many schools as you are allowed to, so you can get an idea of what might be a good fit for your child. Just like any parent with a typically developing child, you are seeking the right school environment for your child's academic and social needs. But your challenge is more complex and your choice of school probably more limited, because you are also looking for a school with the right type of placement and services.

You're Not in Kansas Anymore, Dorothy

In other words, securing services and accommodations for a school-age child is a whole different ball game. You probably found that in the world of early childhood intervention, there were many people waiting to help you and your child navigate the system and services were generously given. And that could also be true for you in your kindergarten transition, depending on where you live, what local laws supplement federal laws, who happened to be assigned to your team, and how much pressure team members are under to cut costs. Enter the room expecting the best but prepared for the worst.

Subsequent IEP Meetings

OK. So my child's now in school with an IEP. Now what? Does that IEP stay in place through high school?

No. The school is required to schedule one IEP meeting each year, to fulfill IDEA requirements. At each annual IEP meeting, a new IEP is issued. But that doesn't mean you have to wait for that annual review if there is a change in your child's needs before that. For instance, what if your 4th grader suddenly falls further behind because of increased reading and writing demand? Or perhaps your 3rd grader's handwriting has improved and is now quite legible, but he's missing a lot of science because of pull-outs to work on penmanship with his occupational therapist.

You have the right to call for an IEP Team meeting at any time, and the school must comply within ten days of the request. In addition, if your child's teacher or service providers see a change, they, too can request a meeting. If that happens, make sure you are present. Remember, any meeting you are notified of and don't show up for can result in changes to your child's IEP.

Likewise, the school is required by IDEA to conduct new testing (although not a full evaluation) every three years, and the same rules apply. You can request more testing or even a full new evaluation much sooner if you think your child's needs have changed.

If your child's placement is working out well and things continue smoothly, you will attend the yearly meetings, request additional testing when it seems appropriate, and work with the team to adjust your child's IEP as needed. In many, many cases, this process works fairly smoothly and keeps the child's education and progress on track. But sometimes, personality differences, difficult challenges, stretched services and tight budgets conspire to cause problems that can hold your child back. Always keep in mind, the law protects you and your child to some degree at every step of the way.

When Team Members Can't Agree

IEP meetings can get very tense when members can't agree. Often, each member is arguing passionately for what he or she believes is best for the child. The most important advice I can give you about difficult IEP meetings is: *Don't lose your cool.* I know that sounds simple, but when you're making decisions that affect your child's well-being, you can become very emotional, very fast.

Approach every IEP meeting expecting the best and being prepared for the worst.

Don't let your emotions carry you away. This is technically a legal process, and it will be solid evidence and credible arguments that will win the day. Yelling at team members will only close their ears to your thoughts, and brand you with a poor reputation that will precede you at subsequent meetings.

Here's a checklist of Dos for IEP meetings:

- *Come prepared*

As I mentioned above, you always want to have loads of evidence and input from professionals to support your case.

- *Stay calm and polite*

Remember, you will continue to deal with these people regularly—and you catch more flies with honey!

- *Stay firm*

Don't forget that the law protects your rights and those of your child

- *Sign only the parts of the IEP you agree with (or don't sign at all)*

Make sure you contact the team in writing to confirm the fact that you either partially signed or did not sign.

- *Do sign the attendance sheet*

This simple shows that you attended the meeting, and you do want a record of that!

- *NEVER walk out of an IEP meeting that is still in session!*

Don't forget, if you storm out or stalk out before the meeting is adjourned, it's still in session! The rest of the team can make all sorts of decisions after you leave. Don't do it, no matter how frustrated you get.

Using the Law to Protect Your Child

There are two tactics you can use to encourage school and district staff to see things your way. The first is using Prior Written Notice. This is a requirement in the law that the school give you notice before changing or when refusing to change your child's IEP, explaining in writing why the change or refusal is being made. So if the school is making a particularly unreasonable decision, simply making the request for PWN can help them change their minds.

Example: *Krish had been receiving OT services at school to work on visual perception issues for a few years. Even though he was improving, he still had difficulty filling in the little dots on standardized tests. Krish's dad spent some time at home administering sample tests and discovered that if Krish were allowed to circle the answer in the test booklet instead of bubbling in the answer, his score improved dramatically. Krish's dad brought the sample tests in to the IEP meeting and requested that an accommodation be added to the IEP. Krish would be allowed to circle his answers, and a teacher would bubble them in on the answer sheet for him. The school staff balked at this; they said teachers are already overwhelmed by test prep and the requirement that they spend extra hours to score tests, and in any case that being allowed to circle in the test book would give Krish an unfair advantage. Krish's dad was surprised; it seemed like a very reasonable and simple accommodation to him. He very politely asked for a PWN explaining the decision. Suddenly the staff members decided the accommodation wasn't such a big deal after all, and they added it to the IEP.*

If the staff members had still refused, Krish's dad would have been able to take his sample tests and the PWN to mediation, and probably come away successful.

The second tactic is taking advantage of what is known as Pendency. This will only be relevant if your child has satisfactory placement and services which the school is trying to change or cut. The law says that if the Team cannot agree on placement or services and you go to mediation or a due process hearing, the child is in 'Pendency', otherwise known as the 'Stay Put' provision, pending a final resolution to the conflict. This provision of the IDEA states that during mediation or a due process hearing, the child remains in his current placement with the current IEP in place. If the changes the school proposes are relatively small and will not save it very much money in comparison to the cost of a due process hearing, then hearing you *ask* for a hearing may be enough to change their minds. And, if they move forward with mediation or a hearing anyway, you have the peace of mind of knowing that your child will continue receiving the services you want in the meanwhile.

Example: *Carly had always struggled with reading. At her most recent IEP meeting, records showed that she had caught up somewhat to her peers but was still about a year below grade level. The school psychologist explained that Carly had made sufficient progress, and that she planned to cut the 2x30 minutes weekly Carly had been spending with the reading specialist. Other children were even further behind, she said, and needed the service more. Carly's parents knew the time with the specialist was the reason for her gains, and they did not want to lose the service. They also knew that if they refused to sign the IEP and requested mediation, and failing success there, if they requested a due process hearing, the case would be in Pendency for quite some time, and at least Carly would continue to receive the service for the rest of the school year, as there were only two and a half months left of school. Then they could regroup over the summer and figure out what to do. But Pendency never even became an issue; when she heard the words 'mediation' and 'due process,' the school psychologist suddenly realized since there was such great demand for time with the reading specialist, that maybe the school should hire a second staff member to come in part time. Carly kept her services and is gaining on her peers.*

There Will Always Be Compromises

A word of warning: there are limits to your protections. Some schools will ignore the law and their actions will be backed up at a hearing; the law does not require schools to give you everything you want, only what the system (or eventually a mediator or judge), decides your child needs; provisions in the law can be interpreted differently by different people; and finally, there is the consideration of how much you wish to alienate the people your child attends school with every day. So if you find yourself at odds with the school staff, always follow these rules:

- Stay polite and friendly at all times;
- Always behave as if you believe the staff has your child's best interest in mind, even if you secretly don't believe that to be the case. Sometimes believing the best of someone helps him rise to the occasion, and if not, it's still better not to insult the integrity of someone who has power in your child's world;
- Keep an open mind. Remember that sometimes you may be in denial, or be too close to the situation to see what's really going on with your child;
- Think carefully about which compromises you are willing to make, but don't make them until you have to; Stay firm and have a potential compromise in your pocket.

When There Is No Appropriate Placement

By the time he hit 3rd grade, Jonas had a reputation at his school, and I am sorry to say it wasn't a good one. Jonas's third grade teachers, a talented but very overloaded teaching team in a crowded ICT classroom, understood his challenges, but were exasperated with him, nonetheless. By the time Jonas's social worker turned to me with his academic records, Jonas's parents and the members of his IEP team were pretty much at an impasse. My findings only confirmed his parents' and the social workers' suspicions: Jonas was a bright boy whose continued high scores on intelligence tests revealed that something in his placement or services was not working well. His behavior at home was fairly benign, and there was no other explanation for the abysmal grades in his transcript. But the school staff was resolute; they insisted that Jonas's behavioral and academic problems stemmed from trouble at home, and that the services they had in place were correct. Jonas's parents requested mediation and while we waited for the date to arrive, I delved further into his records while his parents sought out other placement options. One of the people I interviewed was Jonas's mentor for an extracurricular science fair project he worked on. The mentor was the uncle of one of the other teammates. He chuckled as he admitted that his own nephew had been pretty scattered and disorganized, while the third child seemed to not have much to say. The mentor explained that it was Jonas who organized the experiment, who came up with the majority of the ideas, drafted most of the results, and as far as he was concerned, was mostly responsible for their second-place ribbon at the fair. Curious, I made a date to go observe Jonas in his classroom, and within minutes of my arrival I could see the problem plain as day. The room was crowded with children, and there was a general hubbub during my entire stay. While I was there, two children broke out into a sword fight with rulers, and it was Jonas who ran over, grabbed one of the rulers, whacked it against a desk so hard it broke, and screamed, "Shut up!" And of course it was Jonas—long ago branded as the known troublemaker—who was subsequently sent to the principal's office. How did the IEP Team miss this problem? Jonas has been placed in ICT specifically because of his IEP, but no one had thought about what a crowded, loud classroom would do to a child whose whole day was spent dealing with the stress of Sensory Processing Disorder. No wonder Jonas couldn't concentrate on his work and was always in trouble for shouting at or pushing other children! His placement was the exact opposite of what he needed, throwing him into constant distress. By the time the mediation date rolled around, Jonas's parents had combined my evidence with their own and had found a private school that could provide a placement better suited to his needs. They were successful at mediation, coming away with a decision that Jonas needed a new placement, with a much smaller class size. They moved him to the private school and have requested a hearing to seek reimbursement for his tuition. And Jonas's grades are starting to be a better match for his test scores.

The IDEA guarantees a child with a disability the right to a FAPE–a free, appropriate public education. Therefore, if the school district is not able to provide appropriate placement, it may have to pay for private education.

There are two types of private special education schools. Some schools are completely independent and require payment of tuition up front just as any mainstream private school would do. If the best placement for your child is in this type of school, you will have to pay the tuition up front while you sue the school district for reimbursement of the money. This can be risky, because you may or may not be successful in proving that your child was not offered appropriate placement by the district. What the law considers 'appropriate for your child' is not the same as 'the very best option for your child'.

If cost is an issue, an APS (Approved Private School) is a safer and more affordable option than an independent private school. These schools are licensed and pre-approved by the state for tuition reimbursement. School districts prefer them to independent private schools, because the cost is shared with the state. If the school district agrees that an APS is the right fit for your child, then the only hurdle you'll have to face is the shortage of seats at the really good APSs. But if the district has offered placement you feel is not appropriate, you will have to request a due process hearing, and show up with as much evidence to support your case as possible. While you are fighting it out with the district, your child remains in pendency, as discussed above.

If you decide to take your child out of his current placement and put him in a private school while you work out your differences with the school district, you are required by the IDEA to notify the district 10 days before doing so.

When the School is Not in Compliance

It will be up to you to make sure your child's IEP is being implemented. The level of conscientious compliance from school to school varies greatly. The only way to know that you child is receiving the supports that have been put in place for her are to keep track.

- Keep a dated journal of events relating to the IEP. If something is amiss, note it down in detail.
- Check in regularly with your child's teacher and each service provider, to see how your child is progressing.
- Compare notes with the parents of other children who have the same placement or receive the same services at your child's school.
- Ask your child about his experience with service providers.
- Talk with your child about his school day; listen for comments that reveal the use of accommodations or modifications.

If you believe that your child's IEP is not being implemented properly, first do some fact-finding. Stay positive and ask to talk with school personnel. It's possible that you and they have different interpretations of the IEP, and kinks can be worked out. If you're having trouble communicating with school staff, you have the right to request an IEP Meeting (and remember, the school must comply within ten days), at which you can go over the IEP together and try to resolve any differences.

If you and the school agree on the IEP but differences about its implementation cannot be resolved, your next step will be formal action. This differs from state to state, so call your state's Department of Education to find out whether you should file a complaint or request a due process hearing.

Testing

If your child has had an IEP for a while now and is approaching 3rd grade, you may be thinking about a new challenge that hasn't come up before: standardized tests. You may hear other parents talking about getting 504 accommodations for their children during testing. This is not necessary for you, since your child already has an IEP. Simply contact the team member who usually drafts the IEP (again, do it *in writing* and keep a copy) and explain that you feel accommodations for testing are necessary; if the district representative agrees, the change can be made with convening the team for a meeting.

Supporting 'Twice-Exceptional' Children

Children who are atypical both in their development and in their intelligence face unique challenges without many tailored supports. It is a common experience for these children to find that almost every task they attempt is either laughable easy or maddeningly difficult. If not managed carefully, this situation can lead quickly to boredom, frustration, and despair. If your child is intellectually 'gifted,' enter the IEP meeting with the understanding that school personnel will see his academic success as a sign that he is 'doing fine' and has no need of support. Hold your ground. Show up with twice the evidence. Although it will be a treacherous route to navigate, you will be able to advocate for your child if you keep the team focused on his challenges rather than his test scores.

Finally, I'd like to leave you with a helpful, short overview of the process we've just discussed. The National Center for Learning Disabilities has created a clear and simple 'visual roadmap' of the IEP process. It's a concise reminder of all the steps, and is available as a free download at: http://www. understood.org/-/media/images/categorized/special%20services/iep%20roadmap.pdf

APPENDICES

APPENDIX A

All 220 Dolch words by grade in frequency order

Pre-Primer		Primer		First Grade		Second Grade		Third Grade	
the	one	he	now	of	take	would	write	if	full
to	my	was	no	his	every	very	always	long	done
and	me	that	came	had	old	your	made	about	light
a	big	she	ride	him	by	its	gave	got	pick
I	come	on	into	her	after	around	us	six	hurt
you	blue	they	good	some	think	don't	buy	never	cut
it	red	but	want	as	let	right	those	seven	kind
in	where	at	too	then	going	green	use	eight	fall
said	jump	with	pretty	could	walk	their	fast	today	carry
for	away	all	four	when	again	call	pull	myself	small
up	here	there	saw	were	may	sleep	both	much	own
look	help	out	well	them	stop	five	sit	keep	show
is	make	be	ran	ask	fly	wash	which	try	hot
go	yellow	have	brown	an	round	or	read	start	far
we	two	am	eat	over	give	before	why	ten	draw
little	play	do	who	just	once	been	found	bring	clean
down	run	did	new	from	open	off	because	drink	grow
can	find	what	must	any	has	cold	best	only	together
see	three	so	black	how	live	tell	upon	better	shall
not	funny	get	white	know	thank	work	these	hold	laugh
		like	soon	put		first	sing	warm	
		this	our			does	wish		
		will	ate			goes	many		
		yes	say						
		went	under						
		are	please						

APPENDIX B

Kindergarten Children love action and movement, but they are not always so crazy about sitting still and writing words. When 5-year-olds are made to sit at a table with a pen and paper, many fold their arms and sulk. We don't want them to think that when writing begins fun stops.

ADVERTISEMENT

Children write when they think it has a purpose. Don't "assign" writing tasks as if they were homework. Instead, incorporate writing into play.

Try this: Here's a neat-trick — 5-year-olds love to pass secret notes, so slip your kindergartner a Post-It with a question on it. Do you want a Hershey's Kiss? Your child may write: Ys! You write back: Yes, what? Your child: Yes, pees! Then you can write: Can I have a real kiss first? (Even if you have to read this aloud to your child — or he has to ask another adult for help — you're still teaching the fun of writing and communicating in print.)

Never correct spelling and handwriting at this stage. That will come after your child learns to write words. Child specialists say "invented spelling" is just fine. Your role is to make writing fun — but did you notice how the exchange above prompted your kindergartner to learn the correct spelling of yes?

(/) (/my-school-list/)

/

First grade It's hard to get kids to write with so many distractions. From video games to television, siblings to pets, everything seems to conspire to prevent children from attaining the focus required to write.

By first grade, kids should be writing on their own initiative. How would you like to get yours to write without saying a single word?

Try this: Fill every room with writing supplies. Every parent learns that kids will grab and experiment with whatever's in reach, whether it's a joystick or a box of matches. If paper and pencils are always around, kids will play with them. Put the remote control on a high shelf, and keep writing supplies on the dining-room and kitchen tables.

Long pieces of paper encourage list making. Note cards and envelopes inspire kids to write letters to each other. Hang a paper mailbox on each bedroom door, and never throw away those freebie note cards from charitable organizations — they're perfect for kids who would just as soon write a note to someone in the same room as put one in a mailbox. Index cards, labels, folded paper, Post-It-notes, staplers, sticker, tape, and glue are all guaranteed to lure kids into writing. Second grade Many parents think their kids are overscheduled. After school they have a commute home, a meal to eat, and homework to do — not to mention extra activities guaranteed to "enrich" them. Parents sometimes feel like scheduling writing won't leave any time for what kids do best: playing. How do you get kids to write without feeling like a drill sergeant?

When kids make up games, they invent rules, which should be written and posted. Hang up a whiteboard in the playroom so that your child can write on it as her playing demands. Write this at the top of the whiteboard: "Writing is part of pretending."

Try this: When playing with kids, try to think of ways to include writing. For example, playing restaurant can include menus and little waitress pads. Police officers write tickets. Robbers consult maps of the bank. Cowboys and indians sign treaties. Playing house would include cooking, thus writing out recipes, grocery lists, and to-do lists.

(/) (/my-school-list/)

/

Don't worry if you've never heard of The Penguins of Madagascar (http://www.nick.com/shows/penguins-of-madagascar/). All of today's games are derived from ones you played as a kid. If your 7-year-old says, "The penguins need to spy on the lemurs to bring home the blimp," don't try to figure out what that means. Say, "This spy mission needs a map and a written plan! Write it in invisible ink!" Third grade Kids are so spontaneously creative, but it can be tricky to get them to capture those insights on paper. Sometimes when you sit them down and say, "Be creative!" they freeze up. Then when you let them run around and jabber, suddenly they are producing one unique, funny thought after another. How do you get what comes out their mouths onto the page?

Try this: Give your child a notebook. Kids don't switch instantly from talking to imagining to writing pages of creative stories. An easy way to make the transition is to get your child in the habit of carrying a notebook (compostion books come in all colors and designs) or keeping one nearby.

Every time your third grader comes up with an idea, remind her to write it down in her notebook. Teach your child that her ideas and memories are valuable and collectible and might come in handy for future writing projects — a nature journal, secret diary, spy notebook, and so on. Fourth grade In fourth grade students face the challenge of reading their first textbooks. Where once their schoolbooks were simple narratives with illustrations, now they are filled with bold print, bullet points, photo captions, tables of contents, subtitles, headings, indexes, and glossaries.

The first time a fourth grader sees a textbook, it can be dizzying. This is Big-Kid Land, and students are treated like little scholars. How do you keep yours from panicking?

Try this: Ask your child to pick a topic he loves and write about it using bullet points of fun facts — he can also illustrate his ideas and write captions for the pictures. Whether he writes about whales, outer space, soccer, dancing, or chocolate, all topics can be

(/) (/my-school-list/)

/

described using chapter headings, subtitles, bullet points, and illustrations with captions. (Many kids actually enjoy writing the table of contents, which helps them imagine an outline for their essay.)

When 9-year-olds become familiar with the features of textbooks by writing them, they will find it much easier to read them. Fifth grade If you have a fifth grader, you don't need to be told the challenge is motivation. Many fifth graders think that life is far too full of drama to focus on actual schoolwork.

Puberty is percolating. If your fifth grader has started writing, you may have noticed that, despite your best efforts, his or her preoccupations are disturbingly gender stereotyped. Your boy may be writing about shooting and blood, and your girl may be writing about clothes and friends. How do we get our sons to write about cooperation and our daughters to write about being assertive leaders?

Try this: As much as it makes you cringe, let your boy write about guts and explosions, and allow your girl to write about frenemies and fashion — and by all means encourage the kids who are exceptions to these stereotypes.

The goal at this stage is not to squash their preoccupations but to, as the child specialists say, "celebrate their interests" and get them writing! We'll teach our sons to be sensitive and daughters to be world leaders later, when they're sophisticated enough to care what society thinks. For now, let 10-year-olds write about their interests. Middle school Welcome to the age of protest. Middle schoolers start to look beyond their schools and neighborhoods and think of themselves as citizens of a larger world. And the first thing they notice is that they could do a better job. You may notice repeated exclamations like "It's not fair!" or "That's wrong!" or "Why can't we share our leftovers with starving children?"

The years of self-righteousness have begun, and you will be the focus of most blame. After all, it's an adult world, and you're the nearest adult. As an enforcer of rules, you are the most convenient oppressor. Sometimes even Mom can feel like the Man.

(/) (/my-school-list/)

/

Try this: Don't tamp it down. Use it. Next time your tween starts shouting at the dinner table, listen and talk but also encourage her to get her angst out on the page, even if it's just a private diary. Point out that her favorite rappers and songwriters often write disciplined, evocative poetry, and she should cultivate the same skills.

Kids at this age may be attracted to slam poetry or pop lyrics. If it sounds to you like ranting with no rhyme or meter, don't worry — we're too old to get it. Even if it means spraying criticism all over your happy family, turning your tween's unfocused passions into focused prose is redemptive — and a habit that could last a lifetime. High school The demanding adult world is approaching. Teens will be entering college or the workforce in no time, and they're already thinking about "what they want to do when they grow up." Trouble is, the opportunities they typically see are extremely narrow. They know about your work. They know about the teachers in their classrooms, nurses, doctors, and garbage men. Beyond that, most professions they've familiar with come from the media — i.e. pro athletes or pro entertainers. It's time they understand how writing fits into many professions and encompasses many different professions in and of itself.

Invite teenagers to consider that every minute of every TV channel must be filled by the creativity of writers. List all the ways that effective writing suffuses their lives, on every web page, podcast, radio, billboard, and cereal box. Everywhere they look, somebody is making a living writing. Now let's have fun with it.

Try this: Challenge adolescents to think like professionals with deadlines by offering scenarios:

"You just got hired to write for Jon Stewart or Glenn Beck. He needs a monologue by the end of the day. Pick a partner and write it together."

"Imagine you're the publicity writer for your favorite band. What would you write on their iTunes page?"

"Design your own automobile. Write an advertisement you'd see on TV."

(/) (/my-school-list/)

/

ADVERTISEMENT

"You have to create video game characters and write their dialogue. The deadline is tomorrow! Create your ultimate game!"

"You have to sell a perfume you think smells bad. Write a paragraph convincing women reading a magazine to buy it."

Teenagers can take their assignment seriously, or they can satirize the form, but these exercises are guaranteed to teach them the monetary value of writing.

Common Core (https://www.greatschools.org/gk/tag/common-core/)

APPENDIX C

Kindergarten: Munchy manipulatives In kindergarten, children are introduced to a range of math essentials. Your child will learn to recognize numbers, count objects, and understand number sequence (for example: 5 follows 4 and 10 comes before 11). He'll also learn basic shapes and identify them in his world (for example: "My bed is a rectangle. The sun is a circle.")

Do this: Place a variety of small food items — raisins, nuts, dried beans, crackers, grapes, berries, or whatever you have on hand — and ask your child to separate them into small bowls. Now have your child count three of each of the food items onto a clean surface. How many total items are there? How many will there be if he adds two more of each item? What if he eats two? Make the game low-key and playful. (Allow plenty of snacking!) Follow your child's lead; maybe he wants to shape the items into faces, or divide them according to preference, or stack them into towers. Encourage him to count out the items as he plays, ask simple addition and subtraction questions, and point out number sequences. The goal of the game is simple: hands-on, and tasty, number fun. First grade: Shape sensations

(/) (/my-school-list/)

/

In first grade, your child will hone her "number sense" — her understanding that numbers represent quantity and that we use numbers to calculate "how many" — whether she's counting how many cookies are left in the cookie jar or how many kids she wants to invite to her birthday party. Other first grade math skills include: mastering addition and subtraction up to 20, understanding place values of 1's and 10's, and developing a more sophisticated grasp of geometric shapes.

ADVERTISEMENT

Do this: Make play dough with your child (there are easy recipes online (https://www.youtube.com/watch?v=v_uMnPmwupw&feature=related)). Have your child measure out the ingredients and point out the difference between a teaspoon and a tablespoon, a half cup and a cup. When the play dough is ready, help your child cut it into basic geometric shapes: squares, triangles, rectangles, and circles. Have your child identify the different shapes and ask questions about what makes them different: How many sides does a triangle have? How do you know that's a square, not a rectangle? How is a circle different from the other shapes? Then let her squish all the shapes together into a blob and make her own creations. (For a delicious variation, make shapes out of cookie dough, instead). Second grade: Money madness Welcome to big numbers! Your child will learn about the 100's and 1000's place values. He'll also learn to add and subtract numbers up to 100; count by 5's, 10's and 100's; and calculate standard units of measurement such as inches, feet, centimeters, and meters.

Do this: Create a store by gathering canned items, toys, books and other household objects — or whatever your child wants to include. Then get some play money (or raid the Monopoly box) and write up simple price tags. (For easy addition and subtraction, make the prices round numbers like $1, $5, $20.) Then let your second grader start wheeling and dealing. Tip: Price items on the high side so your child will have to do more difficult addition and subtraction). How much will it cost to buy a $2 can of soup and a $15 stuffy? How much change will he get back if he gives you a $20 bill? What if he only has a $50? Take turns being the cashier and customer, and invite a friend over to double the fun. Extra fun: When it's snack-time, open a café and "sell" apples, cheese sticks, lemonade, and a treat or two. Third grade: Math wars

(/) (/my-school-list/)

/

The multiplication tables are a key component of third grade math, and since they're a basic building block for math from here on out, now's the time to make sure your child learns the tables. (Click here to print out a multiplication chart (http://www.mathsisfun.com/multiplication-table-bw.html) for your child.) This year, she'll learn to multiply and divide numbers up to 100. She'll also learn about simple fractions, how to categorize geometric shapes, and will be introduced to the concept of area vs. perimeter.

Do this: Play "Multiplication War" — a variation of the card game favorite — to help your child learn her math facts. Start by removing the face cards from the deck. The Ace represents 1. Deal the cards evenly between yourself and your child. Both players then place one card face up. In regular "War," the player with the highest numbered card wins the hand and keeps the two cards. The player who has the most cards at the end wins the game. In this version, the player who calls out the product of the two numbers multiplied together gets the cards. So if you put down a three and your child a six, the player who calls out "18" wins the hand. Start out slowly and give your child time to come up with the answer before you call it out. As she begins to learn higher math facts, you can add the face cards back into the deck. With time and practice, your child's calculations will pick up speed. Watch out: she may even leave you in the dust! Fourth grade: Pizza lesson This year, your child will learn to multiply and divide increasingly large numbers. He'll gain a deeper understanding of properties of geometry, including concepts like "parallel," "perpendicular," and "symmetrical." Fractions will also be an important area of focus this year, as he learns about equivalents, adding and subtracting like denominators, and simple fraction multiplication.

Do this: Order two or three small pizzas — or better yet, make them at home with your child. Most grocery stores sell pre-made pizza dough or uncooked pizza crusts, or if you have more time, make pizza from scratch (for recipe ideas (http://simplyrecipes.com/recipes/homemade_pizza/), go here). Let your child choose the toppings and help with the preparations every step of the way. When the pizzas are ready, cut them into different sizes (cut one into eight slices, for example, one into ten slices, and one into twelve slices) and do some pizza math. How many slices are there in each half of each pizza? If you eat one third of the 12-slice pizza, how many slices will you eat? Then use the pizza slices to teach your child equivalents. For example, ask,

(/) (/my-school-list/)

/

"What is larger: 1/8th or 1/12th; 2/10ths or 5/10ths?" Calculate toppings, too, for example, if your pizza has five pepperonis per slice and there are 10 slices, how many total pepperonis? Invite friends and family members to join the fraction feast. Fifth grade: Take learning online By fifth grade, your child should be able to add and subtract fractions automatically. She'll also begin simple fraction multiplication and division, as well as more complex two digit division. A major focus of fifth grade math is decimals: your child will learn to add, subtract, multiply, and divide decimals into the hundredths.

Do this: Your maturing fifth grader probably likes working independently, so reinforce math with online sources of math help and math practice, so she can work independently. Some free websites include Khan Academy (http://www.khanacademy.org/), which has thousands of video math lessons (and other subjects as well) from the world's greatest online teacher, Salman Khan. Sheppard software (http://www.sheppardsoftware.com/math.htm), WebMath.com (http://www.webmath.com/), and Math.com (http://math.com/) offer a variety of math games, practice problems, and math information for a wide range of grades and math levels. Drexel University's "math forum" (http://mathforum.org/) also provides answers to math questions and grade-based activities.

Explore these sites on your own and then with your child to see if they are helpful. Working online isn't a substitute for doing homework, of course, but can help your child practice math facts, find answers to math questions, supplement classroom learning, and introduce the curious student to new math concepts. Middle school: Making math social In middle school, your child will be learning increasingly complicated math concepts. Even if you understand what your child is learning, you may find he doesn't want your hands-on help. This doesn't mean you shouldn't be involved. Talk to your middle schooler about what he's studying in class, go over his homework with him, and if he doesn't seem to be grasping the material at any point, encourage him to talk to his teacher. Check in with the teacher yourself, and consider getting extra help if your child is struggling.

(/) (/my-school-list/)

/

Do this: Participating in a math club or a math circle is a terrific way to keep your child's interest in math from waning during the middle and high school years. ("Math club" and "math circle" are often used interchangeably. In general, math clubs are after-school groups organized at a middle or high school and run by a math teacher. Math circles may be organized outside of the school setting, and are often led by a rotating group of math experts.) Not only do math clubs and circles make learning math both social and fun, math experts say they give kids a deeper understanding of math concepts than they get in the classroom (/gk/articles/why-americas-smartest-students-fail-math/). Find out if there are any math clubs or circles at your child's school, or in your area. If no club exists, talk to school administrators about launching one. You can find more information about math clubs and circles at the American Mathematics Competition website (http://amc.maa.org/mathclub/) and at the National Association of Math Circles (http://www.mathcircles.org/), both of which provide information and resources for getting started. High school: Scope out support High school math varies year to year depending on your child's grade and math level, and is likely to involve concepts beyond most parent's grasp. Stay as involved as you can by checking in with your child about what she's studying. Talk to her teacher if you have concerns. If your child is struggling, don't assume the issue will resolve itself. At the high school level, math classes move quickly, and what starts as a small misunderstanding can quickly turn into a major problem. A single quiz fail may be a major blow to your teen's confidence and without you even realizing what's happening, she may begin to lose her passion for math.

Do this: Be on top of it. Most high schools offer free tutoring or regular math labs during or after school. Find out what's available before your child needs help, so you can jump on it if a problem crops up. Your child may resist staying after school for math help because she's embarrassed, or because she can't stand the idea (what high schooler wants more school hours?) so getting her to go the first time may not be easy. If she goes once or twice and sees the difference it makes, she'll be more willing to do it the next time. Bonus: seeking help for a problem is an important self-advocacy skill — one that will benefit your child in college and beyond!

If your child's school doesn't offer tutoring support, or if it doesn't resolve the problem, consider finding a private math tutor.

(/) (/my-school-list/)

/

ADVERTISEMENT

Common Core (https://www.greatschools.org/gk/tag/common-core/), Summer learning (https://www.greatschools.org/gk/tag/summer-learning/)

Appendix C

APPENDIX D

Parenting (https://www.greatschools.org/gk/) » School life (https://www.greatschools.org/gk/category/school-life/) »
Middle and high school parent-teacher conferences

Middle and high school parent-teacher conferences

Your meeting with a teacher can forge a partnership that helps your child make the transition from middle school and high school to adulthood.

by: *GreatSchools Staff (https://www.greatschools.org/gk/author/greatschoolsstaff/)* |
February 5, 2016

Content provided by: *(http://www.collegeboard.org)*

College concerns? Worried about grades? Routine chat? Parents and teachers meet for a variety of reasons throughout the school year. Whatever your reason for visiting, it's important to remember that you and your child's teachers are partners in helping your child in the transition to adulthood. The combined support of teachers, counselor and you will be essential to help your child get on the right track to achieve his goals.

Your Involvement in School

Being involved in your child's life at school is important. Obviously, you can't accompany her every step of the way, but it's important for her to know you're interested in what she's doing, and that her hard work is appreciated. Also, if you stay informed about your child's classes and activities, you'll be better able to give her help or guidance when she needs it.

Meet with your child's teachers for a brief chat at the beginning of the school year. A good relationship with her teachers will make it easier for you to work together if problems arise during the year. Your child's teacher can also help you understand what your child experiences every day and inform you about her schoolwork and responsibilities.

Talk to Your Child Beforehand

Ask your child if he has any questions or concerns he'd like you to discuss with his teacher and find out what he likes and dislikes about the class. Let your child know what you plan to talk about with the teacher – when your child is involved in decisions about his education he is more likely to take responsibility for his work and performance.

Questions

Jot down any questions you may have before your meeting to make the most of your time with her teacher. Some questions you may want to ask:

- How has my child performed in your class so far this year?

- What skills and knowledge will my child be learning in your class?

- Will my child complete any major projects or term papers this year?

- How do you determine grades on assignments? How do you determine her overall grade for the class?

- If my child needs help, is tutoring available?

- If my child is a fast-learner how can you and the school make sure she is challenged?

- Is this a college-track class? How does this class help students build skills to succeed in college?

- What resources are available at school to help my child with your class?

- How can I help my child succeed in your class this year?

- What resources would help my child do her work better? Are there additional books or resources available at school or in the community that would help her?

Special Circumstances

Aside from any questions you have, it's also important to let your child's teacher know about your concerns or any special circumstances that might affect his work in school. Update his teachers or high school counselor if any major changes occur in your family. Some families are reluctant to reveal private matters, but you might consider simply alerting his counselor or teachers that your family is going though difficult times.

Keep an Open Mind

You may find the teacher has constructive criticism about your child. Keep an open mind to the teacher's comments. Neither your child nor her teacher is perfect, so if a problem arises it's important to consider both sides of the story. The best solution is one that helps your child succeed in school.

Follow-Up

Take notes during your meeting to record important points that were made. Let your child know what you discussed and if you and his teacher made any decisions or came to any conclusions. Set up another meeting with the teacher, if necessary, to monitor your child's progress or to discuss any continuing problems or concerns.

🏷 *Standards (https://www.greatschools.org/gk/tag/standards/)*

About the author

GreatSchools Staff
(https://www.greatschools.org/gk/author/greatschoolsstaff/)

Support GreatSchools in this effort! Donate Now! **Great!** (/) (/my-school-list/)
(https://www.classy.org/checkout/donation?eid=147615)

Join us

- Supporters (/gk/supporters/)

- Licensing (/gk/licensing/)

- Sponsorship (/gk/sponsorship/)

- Advertising (/gk/advertising/)

- Careers (/gk/careers/)

Learn more

- Newsletter

- Privacy policy (/gk/privacy/)

- Terms of use (/gk/terms/)

- About us (/gk/about/)

- Contact us (/gk/contact/)

Connect

- Facebook (https://www.facebook.com/greatschools)

- Twitter (https://www.twitter.com/greatschools)

- Pinterest (https://pinterest.com/greatschools/)

- YouTube (https://www.youtube.com/greatschools)

- Instagram (https://www.instagram.com/greatschools/)

APPENDIX E

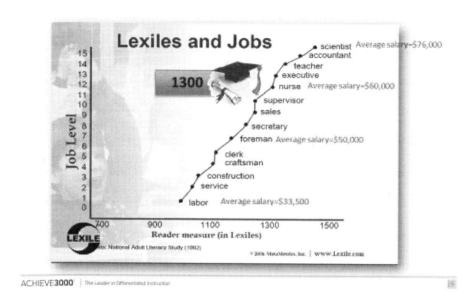

Students Obtaining Bachelor's Degree in Eight Years

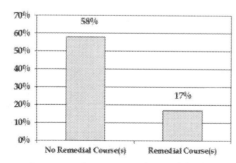

Alliance for Excellent Education, February 2009 edition.

Students who enroll in a remedial reading course are 41 percent more likely to drop out of college. (NCES, 2004a)

Alignment of Taxonomies

Bloom's Taxonomy of Cognitive Domain	Bloom's Taxonomy Cognitive Domain Revised	Webb's Depth of Knowledge	
Knowledge	Remembering	Level One Recall and Reproduction	KNOW
Comprehension	Understanding	Level Two Skills and Concepts	THINK
Application	Applying		
Analysis	Analyzing	Level Three Strategic Thinking	
Synthesis	Evaluating	Level Four Extended Thinking	DO
Evaluation	Creating		

Cue Questions Based on Bloom's Taxonomy

Lower -Order Thinking Skills   Higher -Order Thinking Skills

REMEMBERING
Who (What) were the main...?
What is? Where is...?
When did ___ happen?
How did ___ happen?

ANALYZING
What are the parts or features of...?
How is... related to...?
What is the theme...?
What evidence can you find...?
What conclusions can you draw?

UNDERSTANDING
How would you classify...?
How would you compare...? Contrast?
What is the main idea of...?
Which statements support...?

EVALUATING
What is your opinion of...?
How would you prove...? Disprove..?
What choice would you have made...?

APPLYING
How would you use...?
What examples can you find to...?
How would you show your understanding of...?
What approach would you use to...?

CREATING
What would happen if...?
What alternative can you propose...?
How could you change the plot...?
What changes would you make to solve...?
How can you invent...?

SCHOOL HAPPENS IMAGES AND APPENDICES

https://www.readinga-z.com/updates/raz_correlation_chart.pdf

CONCLUSION

I've had the pleasure of working with countless school-aged children and their parents through the years. Each student I've met has been a wonder to me, a glorious constellation of individual strengths, talents, personality traits, likes and dislikes, learning styles, opinions, ideas, beliefs, skills, jokes, quirks and, yes, challenges. It has been and continues to be inspiring and rewarding to help each family figure out the unique recipe of strategies that set that family's child on the path to academic success and healthy self-esteem. What I've learned is that each child needs a different blend of strategies and assists. This is why I started with giving you context by explaining the big picture about education in the US and then laid out the tools – from simplest to most intensive – that are available to you, so that you can determine which ones will best serve your beautiful child.

You know your child. You now know your options. I know you are now ready to determine which elements from this book, along with generous helpings of encouragement and love, will comprise the plan that leads your singular child to a joyful, skillful and successful experience in school...and beyond.

ABOUT SAKI DODELSON

Saki Dodelson is a renowned leader in the education industry. Saki, the mother of online differentiated learning, was the Founder and CEO of Achieve3000, and co-author of its patented method of differentiation that has accelerated reading gains for millions of students worldwide. She has earned a reputation as a visionary who keeps pulse and evolves with the ever-changing world of education. A trailblazer with a heart, she believes that every child deserves to treated as a "one and only". Saki has been named one of Inc. Magazine's Top 50 Women Entrepreneurs. She is a recipient of the Ernst & Young Entrepreneur of the Year Award, and in both 2018 and 2019 was recognized as one of the top 100 Influencers in education today.

As this book goes to print, Saki has embarked on the next leg of a lifelong journey to bring equity to education and to life through literacy. With the launch of her new company, Beable Education, a new chapter in educational technology and literacy instruction is born. The Beable platform will empower learners to be aware of and confident in their unique strengths and skills. Based on student input, the system will build a profile of the individual's literacy level, strengths and interests and then provide an individualized path of instruction. Content will be tailored to reading level and the individual's unique profile to ensure relevance and engagement and will be powered by a routine that will drive accelerated literacy growth and ensure that every student will graduate "life ready" so they can lead fulfilling lives and secure gainful employment.

ABOUT THE AUTHOR

My first job in education was with Sylvan Learning Centers, I went there one summer to teach and never left. I had found my calling. The ability to blend business with education and creating individualized education programs for each child was in my eyes.......brilliant. Individualized education is the key and schools do their best to support every student, but its just not possible on the level that is needed. Like any other profession, there are extraordinary teachers out there and we hope every kid gets at least one, maybe more. It can make all the difference. But that is not the norm for every student. I loved the whole concept of identifying what a kid was missing in skill gaps and building a plan tailored to fill in the gaps. Just like an IEP for every child. As educators and parents, we all know that every kid is different and deserves the chance to be a productive citizen and get a job. Whatever that job may be.After 8 years of working with parents and being a liaison between parents and school – I knew I wanted to do more. I loved being able to help parents understand how to navigate the school system and support their kids, whatever the circumstances.My next job was with The Princeton Review. I fell into an amazing opportunity that was completelydifferent but perfect for me. I always loved data and have a propensity to understand data and explainit in a very simple way to make it actionable. It just comes naturally. I got the opportunity to managea team and project at the largest school district in the country and build a custom assessment systemfrom the ground up. Design not only the assessments (formative, end of course, summative) but thereporting system and then train the whole district at every level how to access, navigate and use thedata to drive instruction. How to customize instruction to fill in student skill gaps by individual orgroup. It was fascinating and impactful. I was grateful for the opportunity.From this experience, I knew that I could help anyone with school aged children to navigate theschool system.

Not long after, came the adoption of Common Core standards or College and Career Readiness(depending on which state you live in). At the time, I had joined a literacy company that was drivenby their mission to help every student regardless of socioecomic standing or access to the best teachers.We were determined to level the playing field with a platform that was accessible and customized toevery student. It was an amazing opportunity; to get up every day and motivate extraordinary peopleto change the world one teacher and student at a time. There was also an emphasis on literacy andcollege and career readiness which is essential to our future. We were not producing kids even if theygraduate that are prepared to go thru the interview process and get jobs. The greatest gift we can giveto every child is to prepare them to get a job and earn a living wage.

Author available for presentations and consultation services schoolhappens28@gmail.com

Printed in the United States
By Bookmasters